Ed

HERE COMES JESUS

G/L
REGAL
BOOKS

A Division of G/L Publications
Glendale, California, U.S.A.

Dedicated with love and thankfulness
to Dad, Ed Stewart, Sr.
and Mom, Dolly Stewart

Other good Regal reading
How to Be Happy No Matter What (Philippians)
  by Tom Watson
How to Be a Christian in an Unchristian World
  (Colossians) by Fritz Ridenour
Will the Real Phony Please Stand Up? (James)
  by Ethel Barrett
Lord, Make My Life Count
  by Raymond C. Ortlund
How to Be a Christian Without Being Religious (Romans)
  by Fritz Ridenour

Scripture quotations in this publication are from the
New American Standard Bible, © The Lockman Founda-
tion 1960, 1962, 1963, 1968, 1971. Used by permission.
Other versions quoted:
TLB from *The Living Bible,* Copyright © 1971 by Tyndale
House Publishers, Wheaton, Illinois. Used by permission.
KJV Authorized King James Version

Third Printing, 1979

Published by Regal Books Division, G/L Publications
Glendale, California 91209
Printed in U.S.A.

Library of Congress Catalog Card No. 77-90584
ISBN 0-8307-0553-8

SCENES

A Teacher's Manual and Student Study Guide are
available from your church supplier.

SCENE 1: Here Comes Jesus

Read Mark 1:1-8

There was a man who roamed the streets near the office building where I work who made me think of John the Baptist. He wore dirty, rummage-sale clothes and would stand on the corner passing out handwritten messages while bellowing, "The kingdom of heaven is at hand!" Our kingdom-preaching vagrant marched to the beat of a different drummer. He didn't care how he looked or what people thought of him. He was determined to preach the gospel (as he knew it) in the most effective method he could think of.

If there was anyone in the New Testament who marched to the beat of a different drummer, it was John the Baptist. We remember him best for his outdoor life-style and his natural food diet (remember the honey-coated grasshoppers?). John may have looked as strange to his contemporaries as the street-corner prophet did to me. But he was a unique man who played a key role in God's plan of redemption. (Read about the unusual circumstances of John's birth in Luke 1:5-66.)

John, the Forerunner

Mark begins his story about Jesus by introducing John the Baptist—the forerunner of Christ. A forerunner is a messenger sent ahead to prepare the way for another person. Jesus' entrance into the world was so special to God that He sent John the Baptist to prepare people for the Saviour's coming.

Mark dug into the archives of the Old Testament to find two predictions of the forerunner's coming (see Mark 1:2,3). Malachi wrote "Behold, I am going to send My messenger, and he will clear the way before Me" (Mal. 3:1). Isaiah described the forerunner by writing, "A voice is calling, 'Clear the way for the Lord in the wilderness; make smooth in the desert a highway for our God'" (Isa. 40:3). Any Hebrew scholar worth his scrolls should have been expecting the arrival of the Messiah *and* His forerunner as well.

Before John the Baptist began preaching "a baptism of repentance for the forgiveness of sin" (Mark 1:4) in the wilderness of Judea, the nation of Israel was feeling pretty low. The country lived under the rule of the Roman occupation army. The glory years of Israel's kings and prophets were in the distant past. Religious life was mostly hollow and routine.

When John the Baptist came on the scene, some people must have thought Elijah had returned from the grave. John looked, acted and preached like the prophets which his generation had only read and heard about. As he thundered God's message he drew tremendous crowds, because many people sensed that God was speaking to them again through a prophet.

God in General

John's preaching had two main points. First, he came to talk about God in general. "The Lord is about to perform a wonderful deed among you," he proclaimed. "But your devotion to Him has grown cold. Wake up! Get right with God!"

With a prophet in their midst and the words of God ringing in their ears, many of the Jews *did* wake up. They repented—that is, they changed their attitudes about God and were baptized as a sign of their new devotion. Historical sources outside of the Bible tell us that John the Baptist was the leader of a truly great religious movement in Israel.

Jesus in Particular

Second, John came to talk about Jesus Christ in particular. Once the forerunner had turned people's attention to God, he focused that attention on God's Son in human flesh, Jesus Christ.

As the crowds listened intently to their prophet, John would say, "You honor me as God's prophet, but there is someone else coming who is so great that I am not even good enough to untie His sandals!"

Then one day John specified exactly who he was referring to when he pointed to Jesus and said, "Look! There is the Lamb of God who takes away the

7

world's sin! He is the one I was talking about when I said, 'Soon a man far greater than I am is coming, who existed long before me!' " (John 1:29,30, *TLB*).

You, a Follower

You may not feel like dressing in camel's hair or standing on busy street corners bellowing Bible verses and preaching. But if you're a follower of Jesus Christ, your job, like John's, is to change people's attitudes about God and focus their attention on Jesus Christ. As your friends and family see and hear about the purpose and peace that mark your life, they should also be able to say, "There *is* something to live for; there *is* meaning to life. Jesus makes a difference in people's lives."

"How can I introduce my friends to Jesus?" you ask. Take a clue from John the Baptist. Point them to the Lamb of God through your actions and words.

"Jesus has made a difference in my life," you say with your life. "I don't understand Him completely yet, but I can recommend Him to you on the basis of what He has done in my life."

Simultaneously, Jesus will begin introducing Himself to them on the inside through the Holy Spirit. "But when He, the Spirit of truth, comes, He will guide you into all the truth; . . . He shall glorify Me [Christ]" (John 16:13,14). Jesus Christ doesn't crash into a person's life, but gently and lovingly makes His presence and purpose known.

So hang in there. If God can use a strangely dressed health food enthusiast in the Judean wilderness to introduce Jesus to people, He can certainly use you where you are.

SCENE 2: The Start of Something Big

Read Mark 1:9-15

A group of runners shuffle expectantly near the starting line. "On your marks!" Each runner carefully lowers himself into the starting blocks. "Get set!" The sprinters raise their backs and freeze, coiled for the start. A pistol shot splits the air and the runners bolt from the blocks with their first muscle-straining strides toward the tape.

Verses 14 and 15 of Mark 1 are like the start of a race. They describe Jesus' entrance into public ministry. But notice that Mark briefly includes two steps of preparation which Jesus took prior to these verses —baptism and temptation.

On Your Mark!

Have you ever wondered why Jesus was baptized? After all, baptism is the outward expression that a person has turned from sin to God. But Jesus Christ never sinned. Put those two concepts into a computer and you'll get a three-word reply—*does not compute!* Even John the Baptist was puzzled when Jesus came to him for baptism. " 'This isn't proper,' he said. 'I am the one who needs to be baptized by you' " (Matt. 3:14, *TLB*).

Here's a thought that helps me understand why Jesus submitted to baptism even though He was not a sinner: The ultimate purpose for Christ's life, death and resurrection was to provide us with His righteousness in exchange for our sinfulness, right? He identified so completely with our sinful condition that the Bible says He actually became sin, an impossible role for the sinless Christ, that we might become righteous, an impossible role for sinful mankind (see 2 Cor. 5:21).

Jesus' baptism was His initial step in identifying with the sinners He came to save. He was baptized the way a sinner is because He would soon carry to the cross the load of the world's sin. His baptism demonstrated that He was willing to humble Himself even to the point of appearing like a sinful man (see Phil. 2:5-8).

When was the last time you personally thanked Jesus for His willingness to take your sinfulness upon Himself so that you might take His righteousness? Take a moment right now to express your appreciation to Him.

Get Set!

When reading about Jesus' temptation in the wilderness, some people wonder, "If God loved Jesus so much, why did He allow Satan to tempt His Son? He might have yielded to temptation and spoiled everything!"

For one thing, God was not worried about losing Jesus to Satan or having His plan of redemption thwarted. God said to Jesus, "You are my beloved Son; you are my Delight" (Mark 1:11, *TLB*). Satan designed the temptation to make Jesus sin and thus ruin God's plan. But God allowed the temptation to prove that Jesus would stand. He would not sin; thus He ruined Satan's plan (see 1 John 3:8).

Sometimes, when we feel the squeeze of temptation to do wrong, we focus on Satan's purpose in temptation. Then we tend to run off whimpering, "Oh no! The devil's after me again! I hope I can outrun him this time!"

But when temptation comes, if we focus on God's point of view we can say, "Thank you, Lord, for another opportunity for you to prove your keeping power in my life." Perspective is very important in resisting temptation.

Another reason for Jesus' temptation is suggested by Hebrews 2:17,18. It's been said that no one can help an alcoholic like a former alcoholic; no one can help a doper like a former doper. Similarly, no one can help a person overcome temptation like someone who has met and conquered temptation. Jesus knows what it's like to be offered all kinds of tantalizing rewards in exchange for abandoning His devotion to the Father. So when it happens to us, we can cry for help to Someone who has been there and conquered Satan and temptation head on.

Notice in Matthew's report that Jesus resisted temptation with the Word of God, "It is written . . . " (Matt. 4:4,6,10). Every sinful option that Satan presented Jesus was annihilated with the words of Scripture.

You can't be a believer very long before discovering that it is impossible to resist temptation without depending on God's Word as a primary resource. King David gave us this clue for conquering temptation: "Thy word I have treasured in my heart, that I may not sin against Thee" (Ps. 119:11).

Have you ever seen a bee walking sluggishly on the ground, unable to fly? The bee probably miscalculated the distance to a needed source of nourishment and ran out of the fuel needed to power his wings. It cannot fly and will soon die unless it stumbles upon a honey supply.

We are like the bee. Without the continuous fuel of God's Word we are destined to "crash and burn" in our battle to resist temptation. We need a steady diet of the nourishment of the Word in order to keep spiritually aloft. It's a good idea to "fill 'er up" every morning so that you can soar above the obstacles Satan will put in your way through the day.

Go!

John the Baptist, the leader of the great revival in Israel, had been imprisoned. The stage was set for Jesus' debut in public ministry. With two critical steps of preparation behind Him, baptism and temptation, Jesus began His preaching in Galilee. Get ready, world. Here comes Jesus!

SCENE 3: Who's in Charge Here?

Read Mark 1:16-45

When I was an active member of the comic book crowd, my favorite superhero was Plastic Man. He couldn't leap tall buildings with a single bound, but he could stretch, twist and mold his body into any shape —from paper thin to slide under a door, to brick wall

12

solid to block a criminal's escape. He used his distinguishing characteristic—his elastic body—to thwart bad guys and rescue good guys.

We've all followed childhood superheroes like Superman, Wonder Woman, Mighty Mouse or Batman. But in reality there is only one true *super*-man (I say this respectfully) and that is Jesus Christ. He was God in human flesh and He too had a distinguishing characteristic—dynamic authority—which Mark identified very early in His ministry. Though He appeared to be an ordinary man, His authoritative action marked Him for who He really was—the Son of God.

Authority over Lives

Peter, Andrew, James and John, commercial fishermen, were spreading their nets offshore for a catch. Jesus called to them, "Follow Me." There was something compelling about that call because the four fishermen left their nets where they had thrown them and followed Jesus. Think of it! They abandoned their careers after a word from Jesus! That's authority!

It's great to realize that Jesus, the one who calls us to follow, is a truly reliable leader, one who never makes a mistake in His plans for our lives. Have you heard His call in your life? Have you set your personal ambitions aside to follow Him?

Authority over Minds

When Jesus taught in the Capernaum synagogue, His teaching blew the local worshipers right out of their pews. "The congregation was surprised at his sermon because he spoke as an authority, and didn't try to prove his points by quoting others" (Mark 1:22, *TLB*). "Wow, what a lesson!" they must have said to each other. "It wasn't anything like the oatmeal the scribes feed us each week."

The scribes were Israel's lifetime seminary students. They were always studying the law of Moses and teaching it to the people. But often the scribes were so wrapped up in knowing the details of the law that they forgot *who* the law was about. They lacked authority because they were out of touch with God, the authority behind the law.

Jesus' teaching was authoritative because He knew God the Father, the author of the law, personally. He not only taught what the law *said* but also what it *meant*. His authoritative presentation of God's Word rattled people down to their sandals.

Remember the last time you were reading the Bible and some verses seemed to flash at you like strobe lights? That was Jesus, making the written Word come alive for you just like He did for those listening in the Capernaum synagogue (see Mark 1:21,22). He has the authority to penetrate our minds with His Word, teach us what it means and apply it to the nitty-gritty of our daily lives.

Authority over Spirits

In Mark 1:23, the synagogue was still buzzing with comments about Jesus' teaching when a demon-possessed man pierced the air with a scream. He had been undisturbed by the watered-down teaching of the scribes, but the authority of the Son of God terrified him. Jesus openly displayed His authority over

14

the dreaded demon world by silencing the demon and delivering the helpless man from his captor. The synagogue had never seen such authority before.

It's good to know that Jesus has authority over the spirit world, for God's archenemy Satan is still at work trying to lure and control people who give him room in their lives. God has allowed Satan to exert a great deal of power in the world. People who play around with spiritism and satanism are prime candidates for satanic control. But the person who submits to Jesus Christ as Saviour and Lord is under the authority and protection of the One who has already smashed the devil and his God-opposing kingdom (see 1 John 3:8; 4:4).

Authority over Illness

After a day of viewing Jesus' authority in the synagogue, the disciples were beginning to grow in faith. When they discovered that Peter's mother-in-law was ill they came to Jesus and "spoke to Him about her" (Mark 1:30). The Master went to her and lifted the woman to her feet and she was immediately well. Later that day Jesus healed a great crowd of people. They had all come to hear the authoritative teacher. Jesus had authority over the weaknesses of the human body.

You can rest easy that Jesus Christ will not misuse His authority to crash through the doors of your life and muscle in on all your activities. True, He is the only one who has the power and authority we need to meet and conquer all of life's obstacles, whether physical, mental, social or spiritual. But He won't impose Himself on any of us. Rather, He patiently stands ready and available to exercise His authority in our lives. All we have to do is ask.

SCENE 4: You've Got a Friend

Read Mark 2:1-12

"Hey, what's going on up there?" A regally robed scribe jumped to his feet, interrupting Jesus in the middle of a sentence. He pointed an angry finger at a wooden stick poking through the clay ceiling of the crowded home. Other righteous-looking leaders rose indignantly to watch the stick break an ever-widening hole in the ceiling, spraying chips of clay and dust over the people below as they noisily scurried for cover.

Within minutes the onlookers watched four pairs of hands, through the opening, removing roof tiles. Soon those hands lowered into the room a stretcher bearing a man who lay motionless.

The man was hurting in more ways than one. He was suffering from severe paralysis resulting from damage to the brain or spinal cord. The paralytic was incapable of doing anything for himself, utterly dependent upon the help of family and friends.

But his need for wholeness went beyond his physical problem. The story reveals that he was also hurting spiritually. He was a sinner in need of forgiveness.

But let's take a closer look at the four men who

brought the paralyzed man to Jesus. Their names are not given, but we can assume that they were just ordinary men who had a friend in need of Jesus. That means they were just like us—ordinary people who have needy friends. How can these four men help us in our ministry of bringing friends to Jesus?

Faith that Works

First, these friends had faith—high visibility faith. They really believed that Jesus would do something for their invalid friend. Jesus began ministering to the sick man when He saw his friends' faith, "And Jesus seeing their faith said to the paralytic, 'My son, your sins are forgiven' " (Mark 2:5).

But what did their faith look like? Halos over their heads? A large capital "F" on their foreheads? I doubt it. Their faith was much more down-to-earth than that. Jesus looked at the hole in the ceiling, the chunks of clay and dust covering the floor, four sweat-stained faces staring down at Him and a man in need of wholeness at His feet and said, "Now that's faith." Jesus always associated faith with doing something, not just sitting still and mouthing sweet-sounding promises. You'll find the same idea in James 2:14-26 which, in a nutshell says, "Faith without action is dead."

Love that Costs

The second thing we learn from these four men is that their love for their sick friend cost them something. It cost them personal time and effort to get their friend to Jesus. It also probably cost them some money. Who do you suppose had to pay for the damage they did to the roof? Furthermore, they ran a high risk of being ridiculed for their actions. Busting through the ceiling in the middle of a high-level religious conference is not generally acceptable behavior! But in spite of the costs involved, the four men viewed their friend with compassion and said, "It's worth it to get him to Jesus."

The Reward

Finally, notice that Jesus rewarded their faith and love by ministering to their friend. To the astonishment of the self-righteous scribes, Jesus pronounced the invalid's sins forgiven. Then Jesus underscored His words of forgiveness by restoring the man's physical health. Faith and love which paid the price resulted in wholeness for a man with four faithful friends.

You have at least one friend who needs Jesus. Maybe your friend is not paralyzed or living a life of gross sin, but even people in the best of health, living the purest moral lives, need the wholeness which only Jesus can give.

As you think about your desire to bring your friend to Jesus, ask yourself two questions: (1) *Do I really believe that Jesus can make my friend whole?* Remember how the four friends *activated* their faith. Are you actively sharing the message of Christ's love with your friend in some way—telling what He has done for you, inviting your friend to church or Christian youth activities, living a life of love in front of him or her? Faith is shown in action. A lack of action says, "I don't believe Jesus can help him."

(2) *Am I willing to pay the cost to bring my friend*

to Jesus? Remember what it cost the four friends. Are you willing to spend some time helping your friend with a history report to show that you care? Would you pay your friend's way to camp or to a banquet so that he or she can be exposed to the Christian message? Are you willing to risk possible humiliation by standing up for what is right while your friend looks on? Love will pay the price.

Tim is a high school sophomore. He's a Christian and he wants to bring his friend Kevin to Jesus. Tim has talked to Kevin about his own faith and invited him to church a few times. Recently Tim took Kevin to winter camp and he talked to his counselor for over an hour about what it means to be a Christian. Kevin is not a Christian yet. But it is possible he will be soon because Tim has put legs to his belief that Jesus can change Kevin's life.

Wouldn't it be great if Jesus could see your active faith and minister to your friends as He did for the four in Mark 2:1-12? Are you ready to bust a hole in the ceiling to make it happen?

SCENE 5: People Are Important

Read Mark 2:13—3:6

A young couple wandered into our church one Sunday morning and sat down. They were dressed in very "unsundayish" clothes, and the girl was wearing pants instead of a dress. We found out later that they were new believers, having left a life of drugs and immorality to follow Christ.

After the service, several of the church members were discussing the visitors; most were hoping that the couple felt welcome. But one man was silent and wore a sour scowl on his face. Finally he could contain his opinion no longer. "God is not going to bless our church," he blurted angrily, "if we allow a woman to attend wearing pants."

Our dear brother was so intent on observing his interpretation of an Old Testament rule which prohibited Israeli women from wearing men's clothing (see Deut. 22:5) that he missed the true beauty of the moment—an opportunity to wrap arms of love around two people who desperately needed to be welcomed into the Body of Christ. The man was rule-centered at a point where he should have been people-centered.

To be Christian means to be people-centered rather than rule-centered. No one ever lived who was more people-centered than Jesus Christ. He taught, healed, blessed, lived and died for people. He came to help people see that the cold, brittle rules of the Old Testament were basically guidelines for loving God and loving people. But Jesus lived in a religious community that was rule-centered. The conflict that ignited in Mark 2:13—3:6 between the people-centered Saviour and the rule-centered Jewish leaders opened the door which eventually led to the cross (see Mark 3:6).

When the Jewish leaders saw Jesus at a dinner party with crooked tax-collectors and other shady characters (see Mark 2:15), they criticized Him for His unreligious behavior. "Why is He eating and drinking with tax-gatherers and sinners?" (Mark 2: 16). He had violated the rules of their religious game which prohibited "righteous" people from dirtying their hands with known sinners. "We don't party with such scum," the leaders seemed to say, "because we don't want *their* sin rubbing off on *us*."

Jesus, however, saw things from a people-centered perspective. He said, "It is not those who are healthy who need a physician, but those who are sick; I did not come to call the righteous, but sinners" (Mark 2:17). He spent time with tax-gatherers and sinners so that *His* love might rub off on *them*.

Jesus said of His followers then and now, "You are the salt of the earth" (Matt. 5:13). Salt cannot accomplish its purpose while sitting in the salt shaker; it must be sprinkled on the food to bring out the flavor. Similarly, Christians need to sprinkle themselves among the unbelievers in the world in order to affect them. If you have only Christian friends, attend only Christian functions and patronize only Christian merchants, you're missing the opportunity to be people-centered "salt" in the world—communicating God's love first-hand, as Jesus did, to those who need it most.

Jesus and His disciples were also accused of breaking the highly esteemed rules regarding the Sabbath. Over the centuries, the Jews had established an elaborate network of regulations governing what a Jew could and could not do on the seventh day of the week. The legalistic leaders had their noses stuck so deeply into their religious rulebooks that they had missed the entire purpose of the Sabbath commands. God simply wanted His people to take a day off each week for worship and rest (see Exod. 20:8). But the rule-centered Jews had blown the Sabbath all out of proportion, making it a day of "no-no's" rather than a day of rest.

People were more important to Jesus than man-made rules for religious behavior. "The Sabbath is a day to enjoy, not a law to keep," He seemed to say in Mark 2:27. For His hungry disciples out on a stroll, the Sabbath meant picking handfuls of grain to eat even though it was unlawful to "harvest" grain on the seventh day. For the man with the withered hand, the Sabbath meant healing even though it was unlawful for Jesus to heal (work!) on that day.

Even today, Christians allow themselves to be trapped into rules-centered living rather than people-centered living. We decline an invitation to the class party because there will be some "unbelievers" there —and one of our Christian rules is "Thou shalt not party with pagans." We quietly condemn our friends for staying home to watch TV on Sunday nights because some church rulebooks say, "Thou shalt not miss Sunday evening church service." With a rule-centered approach to life, unbelievers soon get the idea that they are unimportant to us or to God until they "shape up" to our religious code. How many people do you know who are turned off to Christianity because all they see in the church is a crusty list of dos and don'ts?

Take a quick inventory of yourself. Are you rule-centered or people-centered? Do your unbelieving friends see you as an open, accepting person or as a

22

lily-white judge perched high above them in a tower of stifling religiosity?

Some of the vilest people in Palestine came to Jesus and were transformed because He was open, loving and accepting toward them. That's the success of people-centered living. Can we argue with that kind of success?

SCENE 6: The Designated Dozen

Read Mark 3:7-19

The movie *Godspell* (a popular rerun on TV around Eastertime) based on the Broadway musical, which in turn is based on the life of Jesus Christ as recorded by Matthew. Some Christians have criticized the film for its symbolic interpretation of Matthew's Gospel. Their criticism is well taken in some instances. But *Godspell* beautifully and realistically presents, better than any portrayal I have seen, one particular aspect of Jesus' life—His intimate love and caring relationship with His disciples.

Mark takes just a few short verses to describe Jesus' selection of the 12 men we know as the original disciples (see Mark 3:13-18). But these brief verses hold some clues that help us understand Jesus' plan for the Twelve, and subsequently His plan for some disciples we know much better—ourselves, the twentieth-century disciples.

Mark 3:14-15 gives three specific reasons why Jesus chose the disciples: to *be with Him*, to *preach* and to *cast out demons*. Notice that the last two are specific *activities* Jesus had for them to do. Like the old, old song says, Jesus called the disciples to "accentuate the positive" (preach) and "eliminate the negative" (cast out demons). But according to Mark, there was a purpose that took priority over these two activities—*be with Him*.

Be with Him

Read those three words aloud, emphasizing *be*. It's important to know that Jesus called His 12 men to *be* something before He commissioned them to *do* something. *Being* is better than *doing*. Preaching the good news and conquering the devil were and are important tasks. But first Jesus wanted a relationship of closeness and personal interdependency between Himself and the disciples. Such a relationship was to serve as a basis for the activities of Jesus and the disciples.

This *being* relationship was the thrilling emphasis of *Godspell* for me. The film vividly pictured Jesus' deeply personal, loving bond with those whom He selected to share His earthly ministry. In the film, Jesus and the disciples travel everywhere together. They pantomime the parables together, sing, work and play together. They're always together. The Christ-figure even develops a personal greeting with each one, showing the closeness of the relationship. As the film rolls the viewer gets the impression that Jesus and His disciples were as close as a group of people could be.

The first requirement for Christian life-style today is *being* with Jesus. Often we are so wrapped up in what we need to *do* for Jesus that we miss the primary joy of His companionship. He loves us because of who we are—His people—more than what we do. Furthermore, being involved in a personal relationship with Jesus makes what we do as Christians worthwhile.

With Him

Emphasizing the second of our three key words, be *with* Him, reminds me of the deists. Deism is a religion/philosophy that says, God exists, but He is not active in the world today. Deists believe that God wound up the world at creation like a clock. Then He went away leaving the world to run on its own. He's not *with* us.

But the Bible clearly indicates that the deists are wrong. God *is* personally involved in His world. Jesus is God in human form and He is intimately involved with those who come to Him. He spent almost every hour of His three and one half years of ministry *with* His disciples—eyeball to eyeball, heart to heart.

And since His death, resurrection and ascension, Jesus is even more with His followers than He was while on earth. Before Jesus departed bodily from the earth He told His disciples, "I will ask the Father, and He will give you another Helper, that He may be with you forever; that is the Spirit of truth, whom the world cannot receive, because it does not behold Him or know Him, but you know Him because He abides with you, and will be in you" (John 14:16,17). Because of the Holy Spirit, Jesus Christ is now *within* us. Because you have opened your life to Him, Jesus is *with* you—in the classroom, at the game, at the concert, in your room.

Him—Jesus Christ

Now emphasize that last word—be with *Him*. The one we are invited to be with is not a prophet, guru, big brother, or hero. It's *Him*—Jesus Christ, the Son of God, the Saviour of the world. Remember as a child how invincible you felt when you were with your father or big brother? How much more invincible should we feel and live because of the presence of God's Son with us!

Do you sense Jesus with you, or does He seem hopelessly far away? Are you knocking yourself out *doing* the Christian life instead of *being* Jesus' daily companion? Look back on the mountain in Mark 3:13-15. Jesus' call for the Twelve to be with Him echoes loud and clear to us today. Relax. Be with Him. And let the doing take care of itself.

SCENE 7: The Sin of Sins

Read Mark 3:20-35

Crazy Earl, we used to call him in junior high. He did the craziest things. He would jump around the campus like a monkey, show up at school with his hair and eyebrows shaved off, and once even leaped off the second story arcade between the English and Science buildings. His antics provided us with a lot of laughs, but I had the sick feeling inside me that there was really something wrong inside Earl's head.

Jesus' sudden rise to popularity in Palestine apparently gave His mother, brothers and sisters the same sick feeling. They were perplexed as He changed almost overnight from a simple carpenter in the quiet village of Nazareth to a renowned traveling evangelist/healer. Jesus' relatives, full of love and concern, feared for His safety and wanted to take Him out of public life (see Mark 3:21).

But another group of people interpreted Jesus' actions differently. The upper echelon Pharisees from Jerusalem decided that Jesus was possessed by Beelzebul (a derogatory name for Satan meaning literally, "Lord of the Dung"). In the course of His reply to the scribes' charge, Jesus dropped a bomb on His listeners when He introduced a subject that has puzzled and terrified people to this day—the unforgivable sin.

Jesus said, "Whoever blasphemes against the Holy Spirit never has forgiveness" (Mark 3:29). Blasphemy is a difficult term to nail down with a definition. Dr. Ralph P. Martin has written some good words of explanation: "Blasphemy against the Holy Spirit is an attitude of resistance to the Holy Spirit, a rejection of God in human life and a perverse confusion of moral values and issues . . . . In Jesus' teaching, it was blasphemy to attribute satanic powers to Him or to believe that He was none other than a false prophet inspired by the devil. To attribute His words of mercy, done in God's name to Satan, said Jesus, is to

27

be morally perverse and spiritually blind. To say that He is the devil's Messiah is to cut oneself off from all understanding of who He is, and so to deny oneself access to God's forgiveness. This is the 'unforgivable sin'—unforgivable because a person like this doesn't know what right and wrong are, and he is in no conscious need of being forgiven."[1]

There are many Christians who misunderstand the unforgivable sin. As a result, they seem to pussyfoot through life fearing that, at some unguarded moment, they may commit the sin of sins without realizing it and be lost forever.

I know a pastor's wife who was spiritually handcuffed by that line of thinking. She couldn't enjoy life because of the haunting thought that she had committed the unforgivable sin as a youth and was hopelessly lost already. She was a failure as a Christian because she could never figure out if she was forgiven or not. Do you know anyone like that? Have you ever felt that way yourself?

What would you think of a shepherd who set bear traps in the pasture where his sheep were grazing? "Oh, I don't intend for my sheep to get caught in the traps," he says. "But if they do it's their own fault and I have to shoot them." That's crazy!

But some believers think God is like that shepherd —ready to destroy believers who inadvertently step into the trap of the unforgivable sin. But our God is the *good* shepherd, and He carefully tends and guards those in His fold (see Ps. 23; John 10:1-18). The unforgivable sin is the *deliberate* action of a person who is so morally and spiritually twisted that he attributes God's work to the devil.

Has this been a hang-up with you? Have you been haunted with the feeling that maybe you have committed the sin of sins and are eternally "out of it"? The fact that you are even worrying about the issue should be evidence that you're a member of the Good Shepherd's fold. The unforgivable sinner, sad as it may seem, has lost all sensitivity to God. Your sensitivity and interest is a healthy sign that God is calling you into closer fellowship with Himself.

If you have sinned, God's desire is to restore you through your confession and His forgiveness. Don't worry about the unforgivable sin. Just being concerned about the unforgivable sin indicates that you will never commit it, that you are where you want to be—close to God.

Note
1. Ralph P. Martin, *Where the Action Is* (Glendale, Calif.: Regal Books, 1977), p. 25.

SCENE 8: The Garden of the Heart

Read Mark 4:1-34

I hate gardening. Oh, I don't mind mowing the lawn or watering the trees. But I would rather take a beating than pull weeds or cultivate soil. In Mark 4:1-20, Jesus effectively used a garden scene to teach a very important lesson. I may not get very excited about raising tomatoes, corn or zucchini in my backyard, but I am interested in the crops Jesus talked about in the parable of the sower, seed and soils.

Jesus didn't have access to chalkboards, videotape units or other sophisticated teaching aids. But He was a master at using the objects available as tools in His teaching. He pointed to fig trees, sheep, water, grain, farmers, bread and other physical properties as illustrations of spiritual values.

Often these common object lessons were taught in parables—simple stories drawn from nature or everyday life which conveyed spiritual truth.

In this instance, Jesus talked about four kinds of soil to illustrate four kinds of attitudes toward God and His Word. Jesus probably told the story as He and His listeners surveyed a field of grain in the process of growth.

Beside the Road

The hard-packed roadside soil represents someone with a hardened life. This is a person who stubbornly resists God and His efforts to gain entrance.

Dave was a guy who was like hard-packed soil. During his high school years he resented being dragged to church by his parents. He knew about Christianity, but rebelled against God and filled his life with as many "unchristian" activities as he could. Eventually the love and prayers of people who were concerned about Dave softened him. The hard soil was broken up and he received the seed willingly. Dave, his wife and children are serving God today.

Rocky Ground

The rocky ground represents a person with a shallow life. This person becomes a Christian but then ignores the discipline of Bible study, prayer and fellowship. He wants the benefits of being a Christian but not the discipline of the Christian life.

Les was like that. He became a Christian while in high school, but when he joined the air force his shallow, rootless faith dried up. Instead of influencing other airmen for Christ as he had planned, Les was sucked into their life-style and withered spiritually. Several years later Les rediscovered his faith and began "digging the rocks out of his garden." Today he is in seminary preparing for the ministry, possibly the air force chaplaincy.

Among the Thorns

The thorny soil represents those who have crowded lives. These people are interested in the Christian life but allow worldly concerns and the desire for material things to choke out love for God and His Word.

Candy also became a Christian during high school. Her professional singing voice brought her much attention and recognition. Though she married and served in a church with her musical ability, the attraction of the world of professional entertainment strangled her interest in God. She left her husband, became involved in illicit relationships and is now far from the God she once served.

Good Soil

The good soil represents the person who has a receptive life; who cultivates an openness to God and His Word. The seed of the Word can grow and pro-

31

duce fruit in the receptive life because the hard ground of rebellion has been broken up, the rocks of shallowness and undiscipline have been removed and the thorns of worldly attractions have been pulled up by the roots.

The good soil reminds me of bright and attractive Donna. She could have succeeded in many intellectual fields. But she carefully cultivated her spiritual life after her high school conversion by becoming involved in Youth for Christ/Campus Life and in a discipleship training program at her church. Today Donna and her husband—YFC staff workers—are positively affecting the lives of hundreds of high schoolers. The receptive soil, plus the good seed from God, has produced an abundant crop.

As you look at the garden of your own life, remember that a farmer is *not* responsible for making seeds grow into plants. He's only responsible for preparing and maintaining the soil. God has endowed the seed with the capacity to grow into a fruitful plant all by itself; the farmer can only manage the conditions of the soil and planting.

Similarly, your responsibility is to cultivate the soil in your own life; God's responsibility is to produce the growth. You can prepare your life for spiritual growth by carefully cultivating your Christian lifestyle—involvement with God through Bible study, prayer, meditation and worship; involvement with other believers through church attendance, Christian clubs, Christian friends. It's a simple agricultural process: you prepare the soil and God will produce unbelievable growth.

Can you dig it?

SCENE 9: Don't Be Afraid

Read Mark 4:35-41

The afternoon sun dipped behind the gentle hills as a small boat carrying Jesus and His disciples set out across the Sea of Galilee. The Master was exhausted from a strenuous day of teaching, so He found a quiet spot in the stern and was soon asleep.

The gentle breeze which had launched their boat quickly mounted to a stiff wind that filled the sails and rippled the surface of the water with whitecaps. Within minutes fierce downdrafts howled through the riggings and huge waves crashed against the side of the boat. The disciples frantically tied down the sail while the boat tipped and rolled over the waves and the water poured in by the gallons. But Jesus slept on undisturbed.

Finally the disciples could contain their panic no longer. They shook Jesus awake and screamed at Him over the roaring wind and crashing waves, "We're about to go under; don't you even care?" The Master rose and shouted to the wind, "Be quiet," and to the sea, "Be still." Almost immediately the killer gale dwindled to a whisper and the vicious waves subsided to a great calm.

"Why were you so uptight?" Jesus asked as the trembling disciples stared out over the tranquil lake. "Haven't you learned to trust your lives to God in such a simple thing as a storm?" The disciples had not trusted God in a simple thing like a storm. They were too worried about losing their lives.

Everyone possesses a drive to preserve his own life. We're born with the will to survive. But the *will* to survive is not enough to keep people alive, for most people have died against their own will. A person's survival instinct tells him to drive on the correct side of the road, to avoid eating anything poisonous and not to touch a live wire. But since human beings are not all-powerful, sometimes tragic events overpower our desire to live. In March, 1977, nearly 600 people died in the fiery runway crash of two 747 jumbo jets. Thousands of people die each year in earthquakes, fires, floods, accidents and other disasters where their will to survive could not guarantee their survival. Even death by natural causes eventually cancels out the preservation instinct.

At some point in our lives, as God's people, we must all learn to say honestly and reverently, "Lord, my life is in your hands." That's one of the truths Jesus wanted His disciples to learn from the storm incident. Nothing that happens to you, including accidents or death, is a surprise to God. He knows what life holds for all of us, including its length (see Ps. 139:16). And since we cannot prolong our lives any longer than He plans (see Matt. 6:27), we need not fear death. The Lord of life says to us, "Your life will not end until my plan for you on earth is complete. Rest secure in that fact."

Eventually the disciples did learn to trust God with their lives. Tradition tells us that all of them except John and Judas Iscariot died as martyrs (John died an exile on the Isle of Patmos), fearlessly serving Christ around the world. They, and thousands of martyrs since them, not only trusted God with their lives, but

34

put their lives on the line and mocked death.

Are you afraid to die? Jesus wasn't angry with the disciples for their panic in the storm, and God isn't angry with us for shrinking back at the thought of our own death. But God wants us to grow in our measure of trust. As we learn to trust Him, we can face anything.

SCENE 10: Tell It Like It Is

Read Mark 5:1-20

Does this sound familiar?

"I was sitting in the airport waiting to board my plane when a gentleman sat down beside me. We began talking and soon I asked him, 'Are you sure that you will go to heaven when you die?' He said he wasn't sure, so I explained the plan of salvation to him. Within 10 minutes he bowed his head and asked Christ into his life.

"On the plane a young lady sat down bside me. When I told her that I was a Christian, she said she had no idea what a Christian was. So I shared the good news with her and she too accepted the Lord before we landed.

"Then there was the taxi driver on the way to the hotel who—"

That kind of testimony used to bother me. Every time I heard one I felt like I was drowning in my own guilt because I had never won a barber, gas station attendant, fellow traveler, or skid row down-and-outer to Christ. The reports from successful witnesses made me feel like a total flop as a Christian.

The dramatic deliverance of the demon-possessed man in Mark 5:1-20 has something to say to anyone like me who occasionally gets overwhelmed with feelings of incompetence as a one-on-one evangelist.

It was a great day for the Gadarene demoniac when Jesus arrived by boat from the far shore of the Sea of Galilee. The man was little more than a vicious animal when he first saw Jesus. But the Son of God broke Satan's hold on the man and he was miraculously restored.

As Jesus and the disciples prepared to sail back to Capernaum, the restored man volunteered to join the corps of disciples. But instead, Jesus gave him an assignment that I think should serve as standard operating procedure for all one-on-one evangelists.

Go Home

The first part of Jesus' instructions to the man in Mark 5:19 was, "Go home to your people." According to Jesus, the new believer's first responsibility was to share his new life with those who knew him best.

This seems to be the scriptural pattern for all witnessing—the place to start is where you live: your family, your friends, your neighbors. Jesus' command in Acts 1:8 gives the same impression. Start in Jerusalem (where they were), Judea (the "county" where Jerusalem was), Samaria (a neighboring territory), and then the world. Christian witnessing is to start at home and work outward from there.

When I was in high school, a few of my friends and I felt very evangelistic one Sunday. We decided to drive into Hollywood (15 miles away) to pass out tracts to the sinners. When we proudly announced our plans to one of the wise elders at our church, he asked, "Why are you driving all the way to Hollywood when you can pass out tracts at the market just up the street?" He saw us abandoning our responsibility to "Jerusalem" for the "uttermost part of the earth."

Another time several of us decided to evangelize the crowds who waited on the curbs all night for the Pasadena Tournament of Roses parade. We prepared some "gospel bombs" (tracts rolled in colored cellophane), drove down Colorado Boulevard and tossed them by the handfuls upon the unsuspecting sinners.

I'm not saying that our endeavors were wrong, but they certainly were not primary. Tracts in Hollywood and "gospel bombs" in Pasadena were secondary to sharing the good news with the people I already knew.

Report

The second part of Jesus' instruction to the man was, "Report . . . what great things the Lord has done for you" (Mark 5:19). Jesus didn't tell him to prepare a batch of evangelistic sermons, memorize 18 spiritual principles or mark all the salvation verses in his Bible with red pencil (although none of these are particularly bad ideas). Rather, Jesus told him to tell about his own experience with God.

That's the basic message of the one-on-one evangelist—what Jesus has done for me! Six-point sermons, underlined verses and witnessing plans may have their place, but the message I know best is the reality of what Jesus has meant in *my* life. When all other plans fail, I still know what God has done for me and I can tell about that with authority.

I thank God for people who can win others to Christ on planes, trains, buses, in gas stations and on golf courses. But most Christians are not gifted in that respect. The first candidates for my one-on-one sharing are those whom I see every day. And the first words of my message are about my personal experiences of Christ's love and power at work in my life.

SCENE 11: How to Handle Hurting

Read Mark 5:21-43

The Place: Somewhere in Capernaum.
The Time: Twelve years prior to Jesus' public ministry.

"Jairus," called a voice through the draped doorway where Jairus waited anxiously. The young man jumped to his feet. "You have a baby daughter, Jairus," reported the midwife who had attended Jairus' wife during the baby's birth.

A slight frown clouded the young Jewish leader's face. "A son would have been preferred," he thought as he reviewed the prominence of males in the Hebrew culture. But then a faint smile erased the frown.

"But she is God's gift to us. Thank you, O Lord, for an inferior but healthy daughter."

The Place: Somewhere else in Capernaum.
The time: Same.

"I'm very worried," the young mother confided quietly to her husband as they prepared to extinguish the lamps for the night. The man turned to her with an expression of caring that encouraged her to continue. "It's been nearly three months since the birth of our youngest child. My bleeding should have stopped by now, but it continues." She started to cry softly and her husband wrapped her in his arms and stroked her hair.

"God has not abandoned you," her husband assured. "I will pray for you every day at the hour of prayer until you become well."

As the years passed, Jairus rose in importance in the Capernaum synagogue and his daughter grew into a lovely young girl. Jairus' wife had given him some fine sons, but their first born, even though a girl, held a special place in his heart. She was approaching her teen years when Jairus heard intriguing stories about a young rabbi from Nazareth who had the power to heal the sick and cast out demons.

Meanwhile, the woman with the bleeding problem continued to flow, and grew weaker and more despondent with each passing month. Her husband prayed diligently and they traveled great distances to consult the most famous doctors of the day. But her hemorrhage continued.

39

The couple had just returned home from another fruitless journey when a friend excitedly told them about a traveling prophet, a young healer from Nazareth who had performed many miracles. As the friend talked about Jesus, a flicker of hope began to grow within the woman.

Jairus didn't suspect that he would have reason to seek the healer from Nazareth, but one day his 12-year-old daughter felt tired and listless. The next day she blazed with fever and the third day she lapsed into a coma. The panic-stricken Jairus set out to find the visiting rabbi and beg His help.

"He's coming! He's coming!" the excited friend shouted as he burst into the home of the hemorrhaging woman and her husband. "It's the prophet, the healer! You must see Him! Come!" Instantly the woman knew that her quest was at an end. She must see Jesus, she must touch Him somehow, and her 12-year ordeal would be over.

The Bible doesn't tell us the life history of Jairus' daughter or the hemorrhaging woman. These opening paragraphs are merely speculative. One thing is for sure: Jairus and the hemorrhaging woman were both hurting and were desperate, and we can all identify with that.

It doesn't take long in life to discover what it means to hurt. There are all kinds of hurt around; everyone seems to get his share. Physical pain from accidents and illness. Social pain arising from hate, anger, distrust and abuse between people. Spiritual pain from sin, guilt, shame and disobedience to God.

Nobody has to look far for hurts. The big question is, what do you do with the hurts when they come? Grit your teeth? Bite the bullet? Hang in there?

Panic-stricken Jairus didn't have time to "hang in there." His daughter's illness was an emergency, so he brought the agonizing hurt of his dying daughter to Jesus. The suffering woman had been "biting the bullet" without relief for 12 years before she brought the shame and discomfort of her physical hurt to Jesus. And they were only two people out of thousands who crowded around Jesus because they were hurting.

Does that give you any clues as to what we need to do when we are hurting? Jesus invited people to bring their burdens, sin and hurt to Him (see Matt. 11:28). He *knows* how we hurt and He *wants* to soothe the hurts for us.

It was pretty simple for Jairus and the woman to take their hurts to Jesus—after all, He walked into their village in person. Jesus isn't here in that sense anymore. How do we go to Jesus with our hurts today?

Prayer

One way to bring your hurt to Jesus is by prayer. Not just the simple now-I-lay-me-down-to-sleep kind. But a gut-level, person-to-person talk with God. Like, "God, I'm afraid I'm going to flunk chemistry and my dad is going to fry me," and "Lord, that really bothered me today when Kim chopped me down in front of Lisa and Carol," and "I feel far away from you tonight, God, and I want to be close." Have a real conversation with God.

Get alone somewhere and tell God about every detail of your hurt. Sometimes it's even good to talk to Him aloud or write down what you are feeling. However you get in touch with Him—*do it!* Tell God in real words just where the hurt is.

Share

Another way to bring your hurt to Jesus is to tell a trusted Christian friend about your hurting. When Jesus said, "Where two or three have gathered in My name, there I am in their midst" (Matt. 18:20), He was talking about being present with us in the lives of other believers in whom He dwells. When you are hurting, you need to get with other believers who can comfort you and meet your needs the way Jesus would if He were here in the flesh.

While I was writing this scene, a friend called to ask if he could come over to my house and see me for a few minutes. When he arrived he broke down crying and explained a family problem that was hurting him deeply. I responded to him the way Jesus might have responded. I put my arms around him, listened to him and promised I would help him carry his burden.

Where are you hurting right now? Have you verbalized your pain to Jesus through a spoken or written prayer? Have you talked it over with a Christian friend whom you respect? These are a few of the first steps Jesus invites you to take toward healing and wholeness. When you take these simple steps, you'll be following in the footsteps of the man and woman in Mark 5 who found healing for their hurt in Jesus' presence.

Read Mark 6:1-13

George and Olive were meant for each other. They were probably the most perfectly matched pair in our junior high school.

George was pudgy, brainy and rather homely. Olive was pudgier, brainier and very homely. Junior highers are sometimes merciless in their verbal attacks on the weaknesses of their peers (or have you forgotten?). Unfortunately, George and Olive provided plenty of weaknesses for the rest of us to shoot at.

One day at school, George and Olive showed up hand-in-hand at the outdoor noon dance and a muffled snicker rippled throughout the crowd at their appearance. But when they stepped into the dance area and awkwardly tried to move their uncoordinated bodies to the music, the kids exploded with laughter. The poor couple ignored the derision at first, but then Olive cracked. She grabbed her partner by the hand and snorted, "Come, George!" Olive dragged George through the crowd and out of sight to the cheers of a heartless student body.

Does that hurt you a little bit? It does me. We may not have the same weaknesses as George and Olive, but we have all felt unwanted, unloved and unwelcome. It is definitely *not* a good feeling.

The story of Jesus is a story of rejection. The apostle John summarized that fact when he wrote, "He came to His own, and those who were His own did

43

not receive Him" (John 1:11). It's sadly ironic that the residents of planet earth in general have arrogantly displayed a "no trespassing" sign to their Creator.

Mark 6:1-6 is especially touching because Jesus is rejected by the people of Nazareth, the town where He grew up. They had heard reports of His powerful teaching and healing ministry throughout Galilee. And His first appearance in the neighborhood synagogue was impressive so that "many listeners were astonished" (Mark 6:2).

"But wait a minute," someone objected. "Isn't Jesus only the village carpenter?" They doubted His validity because He did not have the status or prestige of a Pharisee. He was no more than a common laborer.

"And isn't He the son of Mary?" another questioned. In Jesus' time, a child was always referred to as the son of his *father*. Referring to Jesus as the son of Mary implied that Jesus was illegitimate. The hometown people evidently remembered that Mary had become pregnant with Jesus before her marriage to Joseph.

So rather than welcoming Jesus as a teacher and healer, the people of Nazareth snubbed Him as a simple carpenter and supposed illegitimate. But their unwillingness to accept Jesus hurt them more than it did Him because, "He could do no miracle there except that He laid His hands upon a few sick people and healed them" (Mark 6:5).

When Jesus sent His disciples on their two-by-two preaching mission, He told them how to handle the rejection that they would experience. He told them to "shake off the dust from the soles of your feet" (Mark

6:11) as a sign of judgment against the inhospitable cities. Persons who rejected the message of Jesus would find out eventually that God's rejection of them (judgment) would be infinitely worse than their rejection of Him.

Be prepared to be rejected as a Christian. Jesus clearly stated that rejection, even hatred, would be the heritage of His followers. "Because ... I chose you out of the world, ... the world hates you" (John 15:18,19). When a friend finds out that you won't cut school with him because of your loyalty to follow Christ by staying in school, he may check you off his list. When a group of girlfriends discover that you don't have any personal sexual adventures to boast about, they may leave you out in the cold. Your loyalty, purity, honesty and dependability as a Christian is going to make you look as weird in the eyes of some people as George and Olive looked to us in junior high.

But let's look on the bright side for a minute. Jesus promised a special blessing and reward for those who are rejected as His followers. "When you are reviled and persecuted and lied about because you are my followers—wonderful! Be happy about it! Be very glad! for a tremendous reward awaits you up in heaven" (Matt. 5:11,12, *TLB*).

Anyone can coast along as a camouflaged Christian avoiding confrontation and rejection. But the believer who takes a stand for what is right, even if it means losing his popularity, friends or status, is in line for eternally significant rewards.

How does that make you feel about being a follower of Jesus?

SCENE 13: The Walking Dead

Read Mark 6:14-29

On Sunday afternoon, January 8, 1956, five young men stood on the sandy bank of a shallow river staring into the dense foliage of the jungle which surrounded them. They searched the tropical vegetation for the faces of the notorious Auca Indians of remote Ecuador. For weeks the missionaries had flown their single-engine plane over the primitive river settlement. They dropped gifts in hopes of establishing a friendly contact with the Aucas which would lead to an opportunity to share the gospel. On the Friday before, an Auca man and two women had made a friendly visit to the missionaries' beach camp. Now the men waited anxiously for a second face-to-face meeting with the Aucas.

Suddenly there was a flurry of activity in the undergrowth and several Auca warriors attacked the defenseless missionaries. Within minutes the struggle was over and the spear-punctured bodies of the five young men lay motionless at the river's edge.

The cruel death of Jim Elliot, Nate Saint, Ed McCully, Pete Fleming and Roger Youderian in the Ecuadorian jungle was one of the most widely publicized news stories in the 1950s. Five selfless individuals (and the families they left behind) demonstrated that they cherished Christ's Great Commission (see Mark 16:15) more than their own lives. They were living examples of Jim Elliot's famous quote, "He is no fool who gives what he cannot keep to gain what he cannot lose." (The families of the missionaries continued working in Ecuador and eventually reached the Aucas for Christ.)

Someone has said, "You're not ready to live until you're ready to die." Let's alter that slightly to fit the example of John the Baptist: "You're not ready to live for Christ until you're ready to die for Christ." *That* is something to think about—maybe *twice*.

John the Baptist boldly and publicly scolded Herod for his sinful involvement with Herodias, his brother's wife. Herod imprisoned John, but he still had great respect for him because of his obvious dedication to God.

But Herodias was not satisfied with John's imprisonment and eventually succeeded in having him executed. John had spoken out for God and lost his life for it.

What if God asked you to put your life on the line by doing something like John the Baptist or the five missionaries did? How would you respond? It's not an easy subject to discuss because our lives are very precious to us. We tell God that we will walk with Him, talk with Him, read His Word and witness for Him. That's not very hard and not at all painful. But it's not so easy to say, "Lord, I'll gladly die for you." After all, if He takes you up on that offer it's all over!

But seriously, whether we're able to admit it or not, when we signed on as followers of Jesus Christ we signed on as potential martyrs. Living for Jesus means that there is nothing more important than finding out what Jesus wants for us and then doing it. For Jim Elliot and his co-workers that meant sharing Christ with the Aucas until their part in the ministry was abruptly ended by Auca spears. And for tens of thousands of other Christian martyrs since century one, devotion to Christ meant death by fire, sword, beast or bullet.

Even though following Christ is a life *and* death commitment, probably very few of us will ever be called upon to experience death as a martyr. But we should always be ready for the possibility. Maybe the best way to be ready to die as a martyr is to be ready to live every day as close to Christ as possible.

SCENE 14: I Feel for You

Read Mark 6:30-44

Once when I was about four years old, two of my aunts took me on a shopping expedition into downtown Los Angeles. The awesome concrete jungle was a giant maze of skyscrapers, noisy cars and buses, and bustling shoppers. I clung tightly to the hand of one aunt or the other as they browsed through store after store.

In one department store, evidently each aunt thought that the other aunt had me in tow. All of a sudden both my aunts were out of sight and I realized that I was alone in a strange place. I let out a terrified scream which must have stood people straight up all over that end of the store. Instantly both aunts appeared from around nearby counters and I was "saved." The whole incident took less than 30 seconds (my aunts were no more than 10 feet away!) but the experience of desperate fear has lurked in my memory ever since.

Today, nothing tears me up inside more than seeing a child suffer in some way. Reading about a young girl abandoned by her parents in the center divider of a highway, thinking about the hundreds of orphans left in the aftermath of war, or even seeing a toddler separated from his parents in a supermarket—occurrences like these move me almost to tears.

What word best describes how I feel about children who are suffering? Sympathy? Tenderness? Empathy? Pity? A more inclusive word might be compassion. Being compassionate means feeling with someone who suffers, sorrowing for the distress or misfortune of another, "feeling for someone." I know what it means to feel compassion for someone. So do you.

The familiar story of Jesus feeding the 5000 is a beautiful example of compassion. Notice that the Master's intention in Mark 6:30,31 was to take His disciples away for a brief "staff retreat." They had just returned from their preaching mission "and the apostles gathered together with Jesus; and they reported to Him all that they had done and taught," and they were worn out. Jesus felt their fatigue and compassionately said, "Let's take a boat trip and get away from it all for awhile."

But the crowds followed them by running along the shore and were waiting for them when the boat pulled in. Again Jesus' compassion moved Him to action. He saw the people as lost sheep with no shepherd, orphans with no one to care for them. So He gathered them around and taught them, perhaps about God, the Good Shepherd who cares for His sheep (see John 10:1-18).

By late afternoon the disciples interrupted Jesus to tell Him that they were out in the "boonies" and the people needed to head for the villages for something to eat. But Jesus' compassion also felt the people's physical need. He had to feed them himself. He amazed His disciples by feeding 5000 men (and perhaps another 5000 women and children) with only five biscuits and a couple of fish.

If you look closely, you will see that Jesus' compassion moved Him to do three things in this scene: (1) He gave His *time* to the weary disciples when they needed to talk to the Master, (2) He gave His *teaching* to the shepherdless crowd, and (3) He provided for the *material needs* of the hungry thousands.

Being a Christian today means tuning in on the compassionate heart of Jesus and letting that compassion move you to do something for those whose hurts you feel. Neither the tuning nor the doing are very easy for us simply because our own interests often dull our sensitivity to others' needs. Jesus was a totally selfless individual; He lived His entire life for others.

We are still growing toward maturity and selflessness. Most of the time the needs of others have to be pretty tragic in order to crash through our selfishness and get our attention.

Like Jesus, one of the things we can do to show our compassion is to give time to someone who is hurting. Recently I led a Bible study in the home of two sisters who had just been selected as cheerleaders. Our Bible study was delayed for about 30 minutes by phone calls from other girls who had "made it." Since then I have wondered if anyone thought to call any of the losers or spend some time consoling them because they were not selected for one of the coveted positions.

Another way to help is by giving some instruction, advice or teaching to someone who is hurting. One Thanksgiving weekend our family hosted some out-of-town guests—a married couple, Monte and Pat, and a college girl, Donna. During the weekend Donna told us that she was in agony over whether to keep alive a romantic relationship with a non-Christian boy. Pat took her aside and gave her some loving, scriptural counsel on the subject of Christian dating. Weeks later Donna told us that Pat's concern and advice was just what she needed to let God solve her dilemma.

A third way to help is by giving something tangible to a person in need. Buy lunch for a friend at school who left his lunch money at home. Take a couple of magazines and a bouquet of flowers to a person in the hospital. Give your allowance to a missionary project your youth group is supporting. These are just a few ways of putting legs under your feelings of compassion.

Do you notice that people around you are hurting? Does it sometimes hurt you too? That's the compassion of Jesus rising in you. But don't let it die with just a feeling. Take a clue from the compassionate Saviour and make your move to *act* as compassionately as you feel.

Read Mark 6:45-56

During my second year in Christian college, I lived with four other guys in a college dorm apartment. Alan really impressed the rest of us during the early part of the year with his early morning devotional habits. He would rise half an hour before anyone else, slip on his socks, step into his walk-in closet and close the door. Inside, Alan told us, he would kneel for a time of prayer while the rest of us grabbed as much sleep as we could before scrambling for the breakfast line. We thought Alan was probably the most saintly student on campus until he later confessed that, almost every morning, he went right back to sleep on the closet rug!

Ever since I became a Christian at age 13 I've heard sermon after sermon about the importance of a personal quiet time—a period of time during the day (usually early morning) when a Christian should spend moments alone with God. Just about every sermon on the subject quotes verses, like Mark 6:46, that show Jesus stealing away to the wilderness to pray. "If Jesus needed to spend time alone with His Father," the line usually goes, "how much more do we, His feeble followers?"

Yes, Jesus certainly needed to spend time alone reviewing the game plan with God the Father. I see a definite link between Jesus' powerful miracles (like walking on the water and healing the sick) and His hours of solitude spent charging His spiritual batter-

ies in prayer. Even though you and I may never perform miracles we also need that kind of spiritual
uplift.

When you start asking people about quiet time,
everybody, it seems, has a foolproof method for
meeting with God. Some of their methods have
helped me communicate more effectively with God.
Others have only made me feel guilty because I could
never pray the right amount of minutes or read the
right number of chapters.

Following is my own foolproof method. I think it
will help you because it gives you plenty of room to
adjust to your own life-style.

Get Alone with God

I realize that in our fast-paced, quadraphonic,
thrill-a-minute culture it isn't easy to find a place to
be alone with God. But if you think about it, you will
discover a place where you can be sure no one will
disturb you and God.

In Matthew 6:6, Jesus instructed each of His followers to step into his "closet" *(KJV)*. "But there's no
room in my closet," I hear someone saying. Actually,
what Jesus was referring to was an inner room, one
with only one door. He was simply saying, "Find
yourself a room where other people aren't likely to
wander through and disturb you."

If you have a bedroom to yourself and enjoy a
certain amount of privacy when you want it, that
might be the right place for you to have "alone time"
with God. If you share a room with a brother or sister,
look for another place—garage, den, attic, cellar—

One family we know designated a certain area in

their large backyard as the "quiet place." Occupancy of that spot was always limited to one. For me, my old VW bug is a private sanctuary. Driving alone for 40 minutes to and from my office, I have a perfect time to talk with God. Maybe you need to go for a drive or a ride on your bike or skateboard to get alone. Whatever it takes to find your quiet spot, do it!

When you get alone, get comfortable. Find a posture that helps you concentrate on what you're doing. If you find yourself falling asleep when you pray lying down, get up and walk around the room. If you're uptight, lie down and relax. Sometimes kneeling is a helpful posture when you need to talk to God about something very serious.

Talk to God

You don't need to put together a masterpiece prayer with the proper Sunday-service beginning and ending. Just talk to God as if He were sitting alongside you. Tell Him how you feel, what's on your mind. Talk to Him about your anger, frustration, happiness, thankfulness, anything, everything. You can even say, "Lord, I don't feel like talking to you today, but I will because I know it's good for me." The style of language is not important, but honesty of heart *is*.

You can talk to God silently or out loud. You can write Him a letter, sing Him a song or read Him some Scripture. One high school girl in our group writes a psalm to God every night expressing her feelings and thoughts about the day's events. Use your imagination. Be creative. If talking to God bores you, it's time to find a new way to communicate with Him.

Let God Talk to You

If you give God a chance He'll talk to you. No, not in an audible voice, but through the Bible, and through your thoughts and ideas. The Bible is the main guideline by which God talks with us today. You might want to read a few verses during your quiet time and think about them for awhile. Or you might listen to some Christian music, read a good Christian book or magazine or just think about what God has done in your life. Just make a point to tell Him when you're alone that you are listening for what He has to say to you.

You probably will not be called upon to walk on water, calm the sea or heal the multitudes. That's what Jesus did after His quiet time in Mark 6:45-56. But God does have plans for your life, and you will be better prepared to cooperate with those plans each day after a personal "time out" with God.

SCENE 16: Holy from the Inside Out

Read Mark 7:1-23

While strolling on a Christian conference site in Oregon a few years ago I found a list of camp rules that had been left on the premises by a previous group. I had never before seen a list quite as explicit. The following are a few of the rules from the list. I have written in parentheses some of the comments I imagine the camp clown must have made while reading the rules.

There will be no pinecone throwing. (You may throw bottles, rocks and counselors—but not pinecones!)

Report all accidents to your counselor. (If you plan to have an accident, please be sure that your counselor is present!)

There will be no coupling off in the dark and isolated areas of the campground. (Any coupling off must be done in the dark and *populated* areas of the campground!)

Lights out in the dorms at 11:00 P.M. (Lights out in the recreation hall at 4:00 A.M.!)

No wearing of shorts, slacks, etc., on campground. (Any boys who did not bring dresses to camp will be confined to their cabins!)

Campers are expected to participate in recreation activities. (You will have fun or you will be reported to the camp dean!)

Hands off between girls and boys. No holding hands. (You may hold arms, legs and ears, but not hands!)

Christians have always been good at writing rules. Ever since God said, "You shall be holy, for I the Lord your God am holy" (Lev. 19:2), His followers have busied themselves writing lists of rules, commandments and codes of behavior to enforce holiness in each other's daily lives. By the time of Christ, the Jews had a total of 613 specific "traditions of the elders" (Mark 7:3) which had been passed on from generation to generation since Moses. These were not Old Testament laws given by God, but they were rules and regulations the well-meaning Hebrew leaders devised in an attempt to apply God's law to specific daily situations.

By New Testament times the traditions of the elders had become so ridiculous in their demands on the poor Jewish layman that it was almost comical. Mark 7:1-8 is an example of just one tradition that stated that anyone who was not a Jew was considered "unclean" to the Jews. This tradition required the Jews to wash themselves after having been out among the unclean population. Another tradition stated that even the shadow of a Gentile (non-Jew) passing over their kitchen utensils made the utensils unclean!

Jesus was unimpressed by the Pharisees' and scribes' outward show of "holy" behavior. When they questioned Him as to why His disciples ignored the tradition of ceremonial washing, Jesus quoted Isaiah 29:13, implying that His accusers had a lot of holiness to "show" on the outside, but were far from God in their hearts. The self-righteous Jews were so intent on following their own nit-picking rules that they stuffed God's law—which their traditions were supposed to reflect—into a forgotten, dark corner of their minds.

The Pharisees made a basic error about holiness. By their behavior they were saying that holiness was something a person tacked on to the outside of his life by right behavior. "Obey the rules, do the best you can, keep your nose clean and you'll be holy," they seemed to say.

But according to Jesus, the Pharisees and anyone else who followed their line of thinking were 180 degrees from the truth. The New Testament shows that holiness must be an attitude of the heart before it can be an activity of the body. Furthermore, sanctification, which is a synonym for holiness, is not something a person *does* but rather something a person *receives* as his inheritance by being a believer in Jesus Christ (see 1 Cor. 6:11; Heb. 10:10; 13:12; 1 Thess. 5:23). God makes us holy as a result of our faith in Christ. Our holy actions are by-products of God-given holiness, not attempts to achieve holiness.

The Jews made a similar mistake about sin. To them, sin was an outward defilement such as contact with something or someone unclean. Again Jesus said, "There is nothing outside the man which going into him can defile him; but the things which proceed out of the man are what defile the man" (Mark 7:15).

Sin, like its opposite, holiness, is basically an attitude of heart. Holiness springs from an attitude of Christ-centeredness and results in loving behavior toward God and people. Sin, however, springs from an attitude of self-centeredness and results in selfish behavior which alienates, hurts and takes advantage of people.

It's surprising how many Christians today read of the errors the Pharisees made regarding sin and holiness, shake their heads in disgust and then fall into the very same trap. We seem to get sidetracked keeping our own "holy traditions" while ignoring the lifestyle of love for God and people that is to be the basis of all commandments. Brad wouldn't think of taking a drag on a "joint" because it violates one of his church's "don'ts." But he doesn't see anything wrong with speaking disrespectfully to his parents or hatefully abusing his younger sister. Cindy steadfastly refuses to help her friends chug-a-lug a gallon of burgundy at a party because she doesn't "believe in it." But she tells a boyfriend false, injurious and humiliating stories about three girls who are her rivals.

No, throwing pinecones is not a sin. I'm no holier if I don't throw one; I'm no more sinful if I do. But if my act of throwing a pinecone is prompted by a self-centered attitude, such as anger, revenge, jealousy or the desire to show off my blazing fastball, then I have a sin to confess.

By the way, Jesus did *not* mean that all traditions, rules and regulations are to be tossed out. Rules of behavior have their place and are not necessarily bad (see Matt. 23:23). But if the rules become for us a substitute for the holiness which God produces in our lives, then they have become too important and we could correctly be labeled "Pharisee."

If God has made you holy from the inside out, then let your holy, law-abiding actions show it. And save your pinecones for the bonfire in "Victory Circle."

SCENE 17: Jesus Went to the "Dogs"

Read Mark 7:24-37

"My granddaughter does not need a doctor," the older woman began slowly, her voice rising in anger with each word. "She has a devil in her! She is possessed! No doctor can cure her!"

"But mother," the younger woman replied calmly, "the Nazarene is not a doctor. He's a miracle-worker, a healer, a man sent from God."

"Whose god?" snorted the older woman indignantly. "The God of the Jews? If so, the Nazarene's God can do nothing to help you, a Syrophoenician, and your pitiful daughter. We are only dogs in their high and mighty view."

Both women turned toward the little girl sitting cross-legged on the mat in the corner. Her eyes were wide and glassy, and her head wagged from side to side as she mumbled to herself incoherently. Her hands were securely wrapped with cloth to prevent her from scratching her face during one of her frequent violent convulsions.

A faint smile graced the young woman's face as she turned toward her mother. "But if the God of the Jews is the supreme God, then He has compassion on all His world's children."

The older woman, still staring at her deranged granddaughter, did not smile, but nodded slightly. "May it be so, as you have said," she sighed prayerfully.

These first paragraphs are not found in Mark or any of the Gospels. They represent my idea of what may have happened before the Syrophoenician woman approached Jesus in Mark 7:26. The story is a typical example of the Jews' arrogant attitude of superiority toward other peoples of the earth. After all, they were the chosen people, they were God's children! And as such they treated everyone else as less than human.

But contrary to what the Jews thought, God loves

all people, and anyone can approach Him through faith in Jesus Christ regardless of race, color, creed or national origin. Mark illustrates this truth by recording the account of the Syrophoenician woman and the deaf-mute, both despised Gentiles, whose needs were met by the Jewish Saviour.

Notice particularly the attitude of the Syrophoenician woman. The Jews referred to Gentiles like her as dogs, strictly inferior to themselves. But that didn't bother the woman. She boldly walked up to Jesus and asked for His help. He tested her by reminding her of the cultural barrier she was attempting to leap. (Jesus' comment in Mark 7:27 was not His assertion of superiority, but a reflection of typical Jewish thinking.) But she would not be turned away. The woman knew she had as much right to God's blessing as one of God's "children," and she persisted in her request until she was rewarded. She knew she was not inferior in God's sight.

I know what it's like to feel inferior. Through most of my childhood-teenage years I felt that I was definitely one of God's "seconds, blems or irregulars." In grammar school I was belittled because my name was Edward and because I wore glasses ("Hey, four-eyes!"). In high school I was ridiculed because I was skinny, slow to mature, pimply-faced and uncoordinated. Even though I was president of our school's chapter of a Christian youth club, I felt that the leader avoided me in order to spend time with the more popular, athletic guys.

So by my senior year in high school I had collected a hefty basketful of inferiority, insecurity and self-pity. I was the living example of the chop we used to throw around: "Don't worry about your inferiority complex: you *are* inferior!" Though I was a Christian, I was doubtful that God wanted to trust me with much responsibility in His Kingdom.

But through the caring of several Christians who loved me, notably my youth minister, Dick Ross, I came to realize that I *was* of value to God in spite of my "irregularities." Like the Syrophoenician woman, I began to look past my deficiencies to see Jesus clearly as the One who accepted me because of my faith in Him. He has blessed my life and used me to bless others. He hasn't minded at all that I am skinny, farsighted or named Edward.

More teenagers are infected by inferiority complexes than by any other disease. We all seem to have a hard time seeing our strengths, but we can spot even the smallest flaw or weakness in ourselves with ease. And our peers are not much help as ego builders. As soon as your self-image starts looking healthy, someone comes along and reminds you that you're too tall or too fat, you wear braces, read slowly or play a lousy game of Ping-Pong.

God is no respecter of persons. In Acts 10:34,35, we have Peter saying, "I most certainly understand now that God is not one to show partiality, but in every nation the man who fears Him and does what is right is welcome to Him." That means that He's not looking for basketball stars, cheerleaders, smooth complexions or cavity-free teeth. He's looking for people like the Syrophoenician woman, me and you, who will look past their obvious weaknesses do "what is right," and lose themselves in His all-encompassing strength.

SCENE 18: Show Me!

Read Mark 8:1-12

I had a Christian friend in college who allowed himself to get sidetracked spiritually by a dangerous line of thinking. He told me one day that he· was having a hard time believing that Christianity was true. He said that he needed to see some concrete proof of God's existence or his faith would not hold out. "Why doesn't Jesus appear to me in person or send an angel to prove that the Bible is true and that Christianity is really God's way?" he asked seriously. "I need to know because I feel that I'm missing out on what this life has to offer by being a Christian."

We talked for over an hour and I tried to assure him that the Christian life is a walk based on faith, not on lightning bolts or appearances of angels. But our conversation ended in a stalemate and he walked away disillusioned.

Later I learned that three other friends had each talked with Alan on the same subject. When we compared notes we discovered that each of us had counseled him in the same way—encouraging him strongly to forsake his desire for spectacular proof and cling steadfastly to Jesus Christ as the Bible revealed Him. But our friend did not listen to us. Instead he blamed God for not visiting him with concrete proof. He dropped out of school and began filling his life with activities he felt his Christianity had cheated him out of.

Strange as it may seem, there were people in Jesus'

day—people who actually saw Him—who wanted more proof that He was the Son of God He claimed to be. Following Jesus' second experience of feeding a multitude with a small lunch as recorded in Mark 8:1-9, a group of Pharisees approached Him asking for a sign proving His deity. But Jesus knew that their request for a sign was not to prove Him to be the Christ, but rather "to argue with Him" and "to test Him" (Mark 8:11). They were still trying to find a flaw in Him in order to get rid of Him (see Mark 3:6).

According to Mark's Gospel, Jesus replied, "No sign shall be given to this generation" (Mark 8:12). But Matthew records more of Jesus' reply: "A sign will not be given . . . except the sign of Jonah" (Matt. 16:4). I imagine that a few Pharisees walked away that day scratching their heads. "Sign of Jonah? What's the sign of Jonah? I've never heard of such a thing!"

What Jesus was referring to was Jonah's three-day retreat in the belly of the whale (or "great fish" if you're particular). Jesus was saying that His forthcoming death, entombment for three days and resurrection, somewhat similar to Jonah's experience, was to be *the* sign of His deity. These events would be the sign of signs—so conclusive that no other signs would be needed. Sure, Jesus performed many miracles that validated His claim to being God's Son. But the sign of Jonah was the capstone, the undeniable miracle. The Jewish leaders might have been able to explain away Jesus' other miracles as magic or sorcery. But they had no explanation when the supposedly blasphemous rabbi they had killed walked away from His own grave after three days.

There are still plenty of "show me" skeptics around today—people who challenge believers to prove God's existence before they will admit to the possibility of His existence. Perhaps you've argued with some of them on your campus.

How do you "prove" the deity of Jesus Christ and the authenticity of the Christian faith? Jesus' response to the Pharisees' question about a sign gives me a hint as to my own defense of the faith—the sign of Jonah. Jesus predicted and accomplished the humanly impossible feat of His own resurrection. The tomb was empty. This fact and Jesus' post-crucifixion appearances before hundreds of people can't be explained apart from His miraculous resurrection.

So the next time someone approaches you with the famous "show me" attitude about the deity of Christ, simply say, "Oh I have undeniable proof—the sign of Jonah." After they scratch their heads for a moment, share with them the uniqueness of the resurrection of Christ and the difference the living Christ makes in your life every day.

SCENE 19: No Masks Allowed

Read Mark 8:13-21

Sarah was a tremendous actress—the darling of our eighth grade drama class. She was a natural-born extrovert with a personality as sparkly as a glass of freshly poured cola. Most of our junior high plays featured our bubbly starlet and everyone predicted a bright future for her in show business some day.

Sarah's rise to stardom continued in high school, not only in dramatics but as the center of attraction in everything she tried. In our senior year she was class president and prom queen, and she walked hand in hand with one of our school's most popular athletes.

After high school, Sarah continued her pursuit of success in drama. Her path eventually led her to Hollywood where she appeared in several dramatic television shows.

Funny thing about Sarah, though. Maybe you've noticed it in some of your "up front" friends. I never knew Sarah as a real person, only as an actress. From her flashy "top-of-the-world" personality to her flamboyant signature in my yearbook, we saw only Sarah the starlet camouflaging from our view Sarah the real person.

We are all like Sarah to a certain extent. Early in our lives we learn to wear masks and disguises that cover up some of the weaknesses and faults we don't want anyone to see. As small children we swiped some forbidden cookies then put on the mask of an innocent angel so mom wouldn't suspect anything. As we got older we learned to be more skillful in turning on the charm and manipulating facts in order to get what we wanted and win the approval of others.

Even as young adults and adults we slip into a mask when someone asks, "How are you today?" We automatically answer, "Fine," even when we are "unfine"

—depressed, hassled, angry, in trouble, sinful, hurting. Yet instead of letting people see what we're really like inside, we climb into costumes of perfect saints—persons with no problems, hurts, hassles or sins. Nobody wants to be known as weak or incomplete, so we try our best to show people that we've got it all together.

Jesus, during His boat ride with the disciples, was talking about this trait of wearing masks (Mark 8:13-21). But His often-dense disciples missed the message entirely. "Beware of the leaven of the Pharisees," He told them (Mark 8:15). But instead of questioning Jesus further about what He meant, they began discussing the fact that they hadn't brought enough sandwiches to eat on their trip.

But Jesus was warning them against something much more serious than forgetting their picnic basket. Mark's fellow Gospel writer, Luke, gave a more complete account of Jesus' statement when he said, "Beware of the leaven of the Pharisees, which is hypocrisy" (Luke 12:1).

From the way Jesus spoke, hypocrisy was a four-letter word. Simply stated, hypocrisy is pretending to be something you're not—putting up a front in order to conceal your true identity. The Greek word actually means "play-acting," and originally referred to the Greek dramatists who were famous for their masks.

The Pharisees were such accomplished hypocrites that they could have won Oscars for their performances. Remember Jesus' statement about them from Mark 7:6? "This people honors Me with their lips, but their heart is far away from Me." They concentrated on appearing righteous and religious in front of people, but it was only playacting. They were really far from God in their hearts. On another occasion Jesus said that the Pharisees were like tombs—freshly painted white and kept clean on the outside, but full of rotting corpses on the inside (see Matt. 23:27,28).

Jesus compared hypocrisy to leaven (yeast). When leaven is added to bread dough it causes the bread to swell beyond its normal size. If you study a slice of bread before you spread your peanut butter on it, you'll see that it is full of holes, tiny air pockets formed as the bread dough expanded. That's hypocrisy—full and perfect looking on the outside but riddled with holes and hot air on the inside. Jesus had stronger words for the Pharisees and their hypocrisy than any other human condition. He even stated that He would rather a person be a rank pagan than to pretend to be righteous (see Rev. 3:14-16).

If God does not want His people hiding behind masks of religious piety, what does He want? I like the term *transparency*. A transparent person is one who is completely honest about himself to others and to God. You can see right through him—he's not wearing any hypocritical masks. He's not trying to act out a role which is different from what he really is. When he's fine he'll tell you he's fine. But when he's blown it with God or with someone else, he's ready to say, "Forgive me, I've really blown it." (For a beautiful contrast between a hypocrite and a transparent person, see Luke 18:9-14.)

Being transparent is especially important for the Christian. James says, "Confess your sins to one another, and pray for one another, so that you may be healed" (Jas. 5:16). We all blow it on occasion—angry words, hateful deeds, failure, sin. The key to recovery in such situations is not hypocrisy—pasting on a saintly appearance and pretending everything is okay, but transparency—admitting to God and to your Christian brothers and sisters that you are less than perfect and that you are in need of forgiveness and restoration.

Being a transparent person isn't easy. Jesus was the most transparent person who ever walked the earth and He was treated rather poorly for it. But it's the kind of life-style God is looking for in His people. For you that might mean humiliation as you apologize to a group of friends for a "big man on campus" attitude. Or it might mean embarrassment as you own up to turning in a book report for a book you never read. But that's okay, because the name of the game is not "play the role" but "live it like it is." Can you handle that?

SCENE 20: Will the Real Jesus Christ Please Stand Up?

Read Mark 8:22-30

Interviewer: Hello, radio fans. This is your local man-on-the-street reporter speaking to you live from Main Street. We're out among the citizens of this great land with another man-on-the-street opinion question. Today we're asking the age-old question, "Who is Jesus Christ?" Several people have gathered around me here on the street corner, so I'll begin by asking this stately gentleman, "Who is Jesus Christ, in your opinion?"

Gentleman: Jesus Christ? Oh, undoubtedly He was the greatest teacher and philosopher the world has ever known. After all, He gave us the Golden Rule and that great saying, "God helps those who help themselves."

Interviewer: I'm afraid you're a little mixed up, sir. Jesus Christ never made that statement.

Gentleman: Well, I'm sure He said something like that. Anyway, I think everybody ought to have a little bit of Jesus tucked away in his subconscious. Good day.

Interviewer: Thank you for your opinion, sir. Now here's a young lady wearing army fatigues, beret, and dark glasses, and carrying a rifle. Miss, who is Jesus Christ, in your opinion?

Lady: Ah yes, Christ. He was one of the greatest radicals in history—a true guerrilla and rebel leader. The way He hypnotized His lieutenants into dying for Him, excited the masses, and opposed the system—magnificent display of radicalism. Unfortunately He was some kind of religious fanatic and that caused His downfall. Just when He could have taken over Palestine He chickened out on some religious technicality about being a servant king. Tough break. He let His defenses down and they rubbed Him out.

Interviewer: Thank you, miss. That's an interesting viewpoint. And how about you, young man—you with the far away look in your eyes. Who is Jesus Christ, in your opinion?

Man: What? Oh, Jesus Christ? Far out figment of a spaced-out mind, that's who He is. He's the ultimate cosmic orb, the celestial hyperbole, a psychic generator of the alpha current. Say, where are we, man?

Interviewer: I'm standing here on Main Street, but I'm not too sure where you are. You'd better sit down until you're able to focus on the street signs.

Little Girl (tugging on interviewer's pant leg): Hey mister. Whatcha doin'? You haven't talked to me yet.

Interviewer: I'm talking with people about something you wouldn't understand, little girl. I'm asking people their opinion about Jesus Christ. Now if you will step aside please, I must—

Little Girl: But I have a 'pinion about Jesus.

Interviewer (chuckling): All right, young lady. What is your 'pinion about Jesus Christ?

Little Girl: Well, I don't zackly know who He is, but whoever He is I like Him, 'cause He's my friend.

Whether they're being interviewed or not, most people have an opinion of Jesus Christ. He's been called a philosopher, teacher, rebel, con man, prophet, lunatic and many other things in the 20 centuries since His visit to our planet. Trouble is, most people give their opinion of Jesus Christ based upon what other people say about Christ—historical writings, fiction, the grapevine, etc. They are answering Jesus' first question to His disciples—"Who do people say that I am?" (Mark 8:27).

Remember all those horrible things you heard about Miss Shagnasty, the English lit teacher? "She's a monster; she hates sophomores; her tests are harder than the entrance exam to Cambridge." After a few lines like that, you begin to form an opinion based on what people say. And in your mind Miss Shagnasty becomes a sophomore-hating, test-giving monster.

But Jesus asked the disciples another question—similar to the first, but much more personal: "Who do you say that I am?" (Mark 8:29). In other words, Jesus wasn't satisfied in knowing how well His followers had listened to the grapevine. He wanted their personal opinion based on their exposure to and experience with Himself.

Quick-on-the-draw Peter stepped to the head of the class by giving the correct answer: "Thou art the Christ" (Mark 8:29). In this brief confession I hear Peter saying, "Jesus, I've witnessed your authority over sick bodies and demon-possessed minds, your selfless love for people and, most of all, your love for me. You've got to be the Saviour we've been waiting for!"

Right on, Peter! Even though he misunderstood much of what the Saviour came to do (we'll get to that in a later scene), Peter and his fellow disciples formed a correct opinion of Jesus based on their experience with Him.

Have you ever played the game "Telephone Line" (or whatever *you* call it)? One person makes up a story and whispers it to the first person in a line. The listener then whispers it to the next person in line and so on until the story passes to the other end of the line. The last person tells the story out loud as he heard it, and it's always funny to hear how the story gets distorted from one end of the line to the other.

That's the trouble with listening to the grapevine about who Jesus is. The story gets distorted. To form a true opinion of Jesus, you must meet Him personally through the Bible, personal prayer and interaction with other believers. Like Peter, you will confess, "You've got to be the Saviour!"

SCENE 21: The Way to Up Is Down

Read Mark 8:31—9:1

I can't remember a film that stirred up more discussion, even among Christians, than the 1977 box office smash hit *Star Wars*. Though the characters rode space vehicles instead of horses and shot up the landscape (or is it space-scape?) with ray guns rather than six-shooters, *Star Wars* was a classic melodrama pitting good guys against bad guys, with truth and justice triumphing in the end (hooray!)

The exciting climax of the film begins when the number one good guy, Ben (Obi-Wan) Kenobi, and the head bad guy, Darth Vader, meet aboard the bad guys' space station for a showdown. Each man holds a deadly, swordlike beam of light as they square off for a fight to the finish.

Ben Kenobi is the favorite in the duel because "The Force" is with him. "The Force" is the unseen, but superior, influence in the universe. Ben is the one person who has allowed "The Force" to completely control his life, and as such he is invincible.

As the duel begins, each man chops and slashes at the other with his sword of light. But each attack is fended off skillfully. As the duel between Ben Kenobi and Darth Vader continues, Ben's friends escape from the space station's police force and board their spaceship to wait for their hero.

I fully expected Ben to dispose of the villain, leap aboard the spaceship and blast off with his friends. But as soon as the hero was aware that his friends were safe aboard their escape ship, he purposely relaxed his defense and allowed Darth Vader to disintegrate him with one swipe of his deadly weapon.

"Wait a minute!" I thought desperately. "That's not supposed to happen to the hero. He's supposed to smash the villain, make good his escape and live happily ever after." I was shocked that the invincible Kenobi would give up and allow his archrival to conquer him.

As the film continued to its conclusion, I understood Ben's action. Mysteriously, the *invincible* hero became the *invisible* hero. Kenobi's "spirit" became the agent of "The Force" to ride along with Luke, the younger hero, who led the final, successful attack on the enemy.

Can you see why so many of my Christian friends were discussing *Star Wars*? Perhaps unwittingly, the producers of the film had created a vivid allegory of Christ's mission in the world. (If allegory is a new word to you, look it up in a good dictionary right now.) Christ, the invincible Son of God (as represented by Ben Kenobi), gave up His life in order to save the world. To some, Christ's death on the cross looks like an unnecessary surrender (as Kenobi's death seemed to me). But we now realize that without His death and subsequent resurrection we would be "unredeemed" and the daily personal guidance of His Spirit would not be available to us (see John 16:7). God used—of all things—a science fiction movie to remind me why it was necessary for Christ to take up His cross.

In Mark 8:31-38, Jesus began to tell His disciples of His coming death. But these men, particularly Peter, refused to hear of it. "You're the Saviour, you're invincible," they were thinking. "You're going to smash our enemies and we're all going to ride to glory with you."

That's where Jesus had to cut Peter short and introduce one of the most important principles Christians must learn: the way to up is down. In other words, the way to success in God's plan is not to rely upon our own intelligence or strength to push to the top. That's the pattern of the Satan-influenced human nature—smash and grab, look out for yourself first, do unto others before they get a chance to do unto you.

But Jesus said, "If anyone wishes to come after Me, let him deny himself, and take up his cross, and follow Me" (Mark 8:34). Roughly translated, that means to set aside the primary goal of pleasing yourself first, to accept willingly the unpleasant or uncomfortable situation that may result from denying yourself, and then leave the outcome to God. That's Jesus' pattern for success.

75

That's a very noble-sounding principle, but how can you exercise Jesus' success principle in your life? Here's one simple example:

You and a friend are the last to arrive at a party, and everyone else has already helped themselves to refreshments. Two pieces of cake are left on the serving table—one large delicious-looking piece dripping with frosting, and one pile of cake crumbs which was scraped off the bottom of the cake plate. Peter's idea of success tells you to cut in front of your friend and grab the best piece for yourself. That's the old self-centered human nature at work. But Jesus' way to success tells you to hand the delicious-looking piece to your friend (deny yourself), take the plate of crumbs for yourself (take up your cross) and quietly rejoice that you were able to honor your friend in such a way.

On the surface, Peter's way to success looks like more fun, but remember: after Jesus' cross came His resurrection. After His resurrection Jesus was more glorious and victorious than before. But it would not have been so without the Crucifixion.

If you follow Christ through the Crucifixion (deny self, take up the cross) you are also privileged to follow Him in the glory of Resurrection. The early chapters of the book of Acts show us that even Peter eventually experienced Jesus' style of success. The story of Peter's ministry in Acts is one of persecution followed by triumph through the power of the resurrected Christ. Peter's commitment to deny self, take up his cross and follow Christ was so thorough that, according to tradition, he was crucified upside-down for his faith.

Jesus said, "Whoever loses his life for My sake and the gospel's shall save it" (Mark 8:35). You may never be called on to "lose" your life physically as a follower of Christ. But losing your life can also mean taking a pile of cake crumbs so your friend can have the nicer piece, giving up some free time to drive your brother to piano lessons, or excusing yourself from your cluster of friends to welcome a newcomer to class.

Losing your life through self-denial means saving your life, and that means get ready for some fantastic heavenly rewards which cannot be measured in dollars, popularity or even cake.

SCENE 22: Peter, James and John Go to Camp

Read Mark 9:2-13

"If we could just stay up here on the mountain, it would be so easy to be a Christian. The beautiful surroundings, inspiring speakers, good Christian friends and none of the hassles of living at home. Jesus is so real up here. Why can't the Christian life always be a mountaintop experience?"

If you've attended Christian summer camps as often as I have, the first paragraph is as familiar to you as the pledge of allegiance at morning flag-raising. Perhaps you've even spoken these words yourself. After a week of fun in the sun, where Bible study, quiet time and Christian friendships come so easily, who wants to go back home to the tests, trials and temptations of real life—pesky little sisters, demanding parents, stuck-up friends and school? It's so much easier to live on the mountaintop.

In Mark 9:2-13, Peter, James and John got a taste of the summer camp high, only in a much more graphic way than you or I. As the Master's three closest disciples looked on in trembling amazement, Jesus' appearance was drastically changed. "And He was transfigured before them; and His garments became radiant and exceedingly white, as no launderer on earth can whiten them" (Mark 9:2,3). It was a touch of heaven, just like summer camp.

Then two Old Testament "biggies"—Elijah and Moses—mysteriously appeared and began talking with Jesus as the three disciples huddled and stared, petrified with fear. The Jews believed that both Elijah and Moses were noteworthy among their ancestors because of their unorthodox departure from earth (see 2 Kings 2:11 and Deut. 34:5,6). With this knowledge, perhaps Peter, James and John expected God to sweep all six of them off the mountaintop right into heaven. What a way to go!

Peter, a man who was never at a loss for something to say, stepped forward to suggest that they build three shrines to commemorate the glorious event. But he was interrupted by a cloud that surrounded the heavenly trio. A voice within the cloud boldly announced God's pleasure with His Son, Jesus. Then Elijah, Moses and the cloud disappeared, leaving Jesus and the three disciples standing alone on the mountain. The mountaintop experience ended.

Isn't that the way it is at camp? Great music, inspiring speakers, heavenly atmosphere—Christianity couldn't be easier! On Saturday you ride down the mountain singing camp songs until you're hoarse. On Sunday you give a glowing testimony of your fresh commitment to Christ, and everything is rosy and bright—heavenly!

But then, thud! Monday morning. Your alarm nags you out of bed, the clothes you want to wear are still dirty from camp, you discover three new pimples and you're served oatmeal for breakfast. The thrill is gone! Camp is over! Life with all its disgusting realities and complexities is back. Yuk!

But that's the way it is after a spiritual high like camp. It's happened to me and almost every teenager I've ever known. The only people who get to stay on the mountaintop are the camp staff. For everyone else, it's back to the nasty here-and-now.

But wait a minute! Take a look back up on the mountain in Mark 9:9. There are *four* figures winding their way back to the valley from the mountaintop experience. Peter, James, John—and Jesus! It's not Jesus in shining robes, flanked by Elijah and Moses, and wreathed by a heavenly, talking cloud. No, it's Jesus in everyday clothes, walking in shoulder-rubbing closeness to His friends as He accompanies them back to the nasty here-and-now.

That's what we tend to forget when coming back from camp, church, Christian club meeting or any other mountaintop experience. Jesus is not confined to a mountaintop lodge, chapel or sanctuary. He journeys with us into everyday life to help us with nagging alarms, pimples and gooey oatmeal.

It's great to journey to a mountaintop and get a glimpse of a gloriously glowing Jesus. These occasional experiences with Christ help charge our spiritual batteries. But everyday life is in the trenches and the valleys, not on the mountaintop. And that's where Jesus is today—right here in the valleys with you, helping you to live out the mountaintop glow.

Do you see Him?

SCENE 23: I Believe, Sometimes

Read Mark 9:14-29

"Why can't you do something for the boy?" The scribe screams his taunt at the nine disciples who huddle together like frightened puppies. "You say you are the followers of the Rabbi, that He has given you power to deliver the demon-possessed, but there you stand powerless while the boy and his father suffer. Let's see some action here or stop all this pompous talk about being followers of the Son of God!"

The scribe waves his arms wildly as he concludes his accusation. Several other leaders hurl their abusive comments at the disciples as a growing crowd restlessly add an "amen."

Meanwhile, in the shadows, almost overlooked in all the furor, stands a sorrowful looking man with his arms wrapped around a pale, thin boy with dark eyes and unkempt hair. Tears streak the father's weathered face as he watches the disciples try to explain their ineffectiveness to the scribes. The boy rests his head on his father's chest—a blank stare in his shadowy eyes and saliva dripping from his chin.

Suddenly the argument stops. The crowd hushes as it turns in the direction of four approaching men—Peter, James, John and Jesus. Recognizing Jesus, the father half-carries, half-drags his son forward and tells Him the story behind the argument. As Jesus draws near the boy stiffens and moans, and the evil spirit within him wrenches him into violent convulsions.

"Take pity on us and help us!" (Mark 9:22) the father cries helplessly. Jesus encourages the man to have faith, to believe in Him. But the confused father sobs the immortal words that describe the state of faith in most Christians: "I do believe; help me in my unbelief" (Mark 9:24).

That sounds like a contradictory statement, doesn't it? But I can identify with that man as I hear him say, "Lord, I believe in you and your power. But I'm having trouble believing in you for this particular situation. Help me in this area of my faith." The statement is not contradictory—it's reality! And Jesus responded by delivering the boy.

Faith, in simple terms, is the ability to see and act upon what God can do in a certain situation. Kim can "see" her friend Robin coming to Christ in the future, so she prays for Robin and invites her often to a campus Bible study. Cal "sees" God active in his life as a result of his personal quiet time, so he spends 10-15 minutes each morning reading the Word and talking to God in prayer. Faith looks ahead to see what God wants to do and then acts on what it sees.

Faith is like the pitcher on a baseball team—you really can't play the game without him. The Bible uses strong words to describe the role of faith in the Christian life: "Without faith it is impossible to please [God]" (Heb. 11:6); "The righteous man shall live by faith" (Rom. 1:17); "Whatever is not from faith is sin" (Rom. 14:23). The apostle Paul said faith was one of the three great qualities in the Christian life— the others being hope and love (see 1 Cor. 13:13). Yes, faith is indispensable.

But faith is also elusive, as Mark 9:24 illustrates. There are times when your faith can look ahead and see God at work, and there are times when the eyelids of doubt, worry or spiritual ignorance droop across the eyes of faith, blinding you to what God wants to do. The father in Mark 9 could see God doing some things, but he couldn't see his boy being delivered from the evil spirit.

Kim can see Robin becoming a Christian, but she has difficulty seeing God at work in her studies, so she worries about grades constantly. Cal sees God at work as a result of his quiet time, but sometimes he is unable to see God's provision for his financial needs, so he seldom gives any of his hard-earned cash to God in the church offering.

Yes, faith is sometimes like the old shell game— now you see it, now you don't. Sometimes I'm able to exclaim, "I do believe!" But at other times I beg God to "help me in my unbelief." And if you feel that way too, take heart. It's a confession that is common to all members of God's family.

Two encouraging messages about faith from God's Word flash as brightly as neon signs for me. The first is that God is the one who deals out faith to begin with (see Rom. 12:3). I can't earn it or buy it—God gives it.

Second, faith grows in proportion to my relationship with the Word of God (see Rom. 10:17). I can expect my faith to grow toward "I do believe" and away from "Help me in my unbelief" as I relate myself to God's Word through reading, studying, memorizing and sharing the Bible.

It assures me to know that even Jesus' disciples, though they watched Him minister for three years, were often short on faith. Perhaps you, like me, are painfully aware of your need to grow as men and women of faith. All together now, let's join in reciting the disciple's prayer on this subject.

Ready, begin.

"Lord, increase our faith" (Luke 17:5, *KJV*).

SCENE 24: The Jesus University of the Road

Read Mark 9:30-50

One of the highlights of my grammar school career was going on field trips. I lived for the days when the teacher would lead our class across the schoolyard and onto the bus for a day of learning on the road. In class we could only listen as the teacher droned on about California history. But on a field trip to one of the crusty old adobe missions, we saw and felt our history lesson. The subject of science had little attraction for me in the classroom. But when our class traveled to the observatory or the museum of science and industry, science came alive in the wonderland of models, demonstrations and "do-it-yourself" experiments.

In a sense, the three years Jesus spent with His disciples were one long field trip. The men to whom Jesus said "Follow Me," journeyed with the Master throughout Palestine, and every bend in the road and personal encounter was a learning experience.

Of the four Gospels, Mark puts the greatest emphasis on Jesus' actions. Mark saw the Jesus University of the Road as a school that taught by action more than by words. But in this scene, the Gospel writer recalls a handful of mini-lectures Jesus delivered to His 12 followers on the road. Let's review some of the courses He offered in this Scripture section.

Doctrine of Future Things 101 (vv. 30-32)

The disciples failed the course on future things repeatedly. Jesus, for the second time, explained the three-step climax to His earthly ministry: "The Son of Man is to be delivered up into the hands of men, and they will kill Him; and . . . He will rise again three days later" (Mark 9:31). But the disciples were so blinded by their own notion of what the Messiah was supposed to be like—a cross between Moses and Alexander the Great—that Jesus' prediction did not compute.

Perhaps you had similar notions about your dad when you were a child. In your eyes, your father was invincible—he could do *anything*. Your innocent, childish mind couldn't even imagine that he had any weaknesses.

The disciples seemed to see Jesus through those eyes of innocence. The idea that He could be rejected and killed was unthinkable. Therefore, they couldn't comprehend that He would "rise again three days later." "They did not understand this statement" (Mark 9:32), and the thought frightened them to the point that they were unable to ask Him what He meant.

Interpersonal Relationships 106 (vv. 33-37)

Any ideas that Jesus selected the 12 disciples because they were flawless specimens of spiritual activity are blown away by the description of their behavior in these verses. They were instead perfect examples of the human race—proud, boastful and self-centered. With a supposed world leader in their midst, the men were quietly scrambling for top positions in His cabinet as they "discussed with one another which of them was the greatest" (Mark 9:34).

Jesus responded to man's struggle for greatness with some well-chosen words and a life full of action. His words are summarized in Mark 9:35, "If anyone wants to be first, he shall be last of all, and servant of all." Jesus' actions were summarized, in John 13:1-17, when He washed His disciples' feet to demonstrate greatness in God's Kingdom.

The person who pushes others beneath him to appear great is going the wrong direction. Jesus says that the person who kneels before others in order to serve them has found the path to true greatness (see scene 21).

Denominational Distinctives 303 (vv. 38-42)

The apostle John was really shook up. He saw someone else minister to people in Christ's name; then he tried to shut him down because "he was not following us" (Mark 9:38). "Hey, you can't do that," John might have said. "You're not a card-carrying disciple. Besides, you didn't exorcise the demon our way; you don't dress like we do and you say *ay*-men instead of *ah*-men at the end of your prayers."

What I hear Jesus saying in His reply is, "It's okay, John. Just because he's not in your denomination doesn't mean he isn't one of my disciples. The important thing isn't that he be in our group but that he minister in my name."

There are a lot of people around today who think as John thought. We know the Bible says that all believers are one in Christ, but we are pretty suspicious of anybody who doesn't believe in Christ exactly the way we were taught.

Greg, Bob and Eric are all Christians. Each has invited Christ to be the Lord of his life and all three will enjoy heaven together.

Greg's church has a narthex and chancel; the congregation sings anthems for worship; the ministers serve wine for communion and baptize by sprinkling. Bob's church has a foyer and choir loft; the congregation sings gospel songs in worship; the pastors serve grape juice for communion and baptize by immersion (dipping under water). Eric's church meets in a home, the believers sing only Scripture songs, and the elders serve Hawaiian punch (or whatever else is handy) for communion and baptize in a swimming pool by whatever method the convert desires.

If these three guys attended the same school they could do one of two things: (1) avoid each other suspiciously and seek Christian fellowship with their own "kind," or (2) set their denominational distinctives aside and focus on their oneness in Christ. Jesus' model in Mark 9:38-42 leads me to believe that He preferred the latter.

It's important for Jesus' followers around the world to reach past some of their church traditions and distinctives to link hands and hearts as one in Christ. As long as someone claims a relationship to God through faith in Christ as Saviour there is common ground upon which to build a relationship. We are not to let modes of worship or denominational distinctives separate us as family members.

Spiritual Physiology 215 (vv. 43-50)

I read the story in the newspaper with my own eyes, but I could hardly believe what I read. Two policemen spotted a young man staggering along the roadside carrying a Bible under one arm. The other arm was tucked tightly under the Bible in an attempt to stem the flow of heavy bleeding where the man had cut off his own hand! The policemen retrieved the severed hand from a trash can and doctors sewed it back on his arm. The young man said he cut off his hand to obey Mark 9:43, "If your hand causes you to stumble, cut it off."

This section of Scripture is a good illustration that

87

people need to know what the Bible *means*, not just what it *says*. If Jesus' commands in Mark 9:43-50 were to be taken literally, every believer alive would need to schedule himself for several amputations. Which of us has never sinned with our eyes (lusting, coveting), hands (stealing, hitting) or feet (walking into trouble)? If we all did precisely what the Bible *said* in this case, we would need to rewrite the Christian folk hymn to read, "And they'll know we are Christians by our stumps!"

Jesus was using a device known as hyperbole (high-per-boe-lee), exaggeration for effect and emphasis. You hear hyperbole every day: "I've told you a *million* times; I was so embarrassed I could have *died*; I'm so hungry I could eat a *horse*; he's as big as an *ox*." The statements are not literally true but are overstated to drive home a point.

The point Jesus was driving home was that there are two ways to use your physical body—*for* God's purposes or *against* God's purposes. If your goal is to serve God, and yet you let your body do things that do not please God, your body is your enemy. Jesus wants you, His followers, to give your eyes, hands and feet (and everything else for that matter) to Him as well as your soul.

Paul said it this way: "I urge you therefore, brethren ... to present your bodies ... to God" (Rom. 12:1). God is not interested in watching people chop themselves to sinlessness, but rather He wants them to discipline their physical bodies to match their spiritual commitment.

It would have been nice to wander through Palestine with the Jesus University of the Road, hearing firsthand what the Master said and quizzing Him about what He meant. But here's some good news: wherever we go His Spirit is within us and His Word is before us. That means that the Jesus University of the Road is in session wherever you let Christ walk with you. And that's a lot handier than going to Palestine.

SCENE 25: Divorce Is a Four-Letter Word

Read Mark 10:1-12

Mike and Diane, both high school students, met in the market where they worked as clerks. They began dating and soon fell madly in love. From then on Mike and Diane were inseparable—even stealing moments at the market to meet in the stockroom for sweet words and kisses.

They married before graduation and Diane gave birth to a baby within the first year of marriage. But during the second year, Mike and Diane fell out of love almost as quickly as they fell in. They ended their Cinderella romance with a divorce.

Similar things happened to Biff and Karen, Ted and Linda, and Kurt and Gail. Each couple met, fell in love, married, fell out of love and divorced—some with children, some without.

Every person reading this page can easily think of

at least one couple that has become victims of the divorce epidemic: acquaintances, neighbors, friends and possibly even parents. Divorce even happens among Christians. Three out of the four couples named above professed to be devout believers. But when you bring up the subject of divorce in church, watch out! It's a controversial topic among Christians.

Divorce Is a Dirty Word

The subject of divorce was a hot issue in Jesus' day too. According to the Old Testament, a man could divorce his wife when "she finds no favor in his eyes because he has found some indecency in her" (Deut. 24:1). But by the time Jesus came there were two conflicting views about divorce among the Jews, stemming from two interpretations of the word "indecency" in Deuteronomy 24:1. The Pharisees, hard-nosed sticklers for detail, said that indecency referred only to sexual unfaithfulness—a man could divorce his wife only if she became sexually involved with another man.

A second view interpreted "indecency" as *anything* that displeased the husband. A man could divorce his wife for such a simple offense as burning his toast or losing his sock in the laundromat! Herod, the immoral Jewish king, liked this interpretation because it gave him an easy way out of his marriage.

The Pharisees asked Jesus what was His interpretation of divorce (see Mark 10:2) in order to find some reason to accuse Him and get rid of Him (something they had been trying to do since Mark 3:6). The Pharisees were probably hoping that Jesus held the lenient view of divorce; that way they could discredit Him among the religious community for His liberal interpretation of Scripture.

But once again Jesus turned the tables on His enemies in their attempt to trap Him. Instead of siding with one of the two views, Jesus stated that, in God's view of marriage, divorce is a dirty word. Jesus quoted God's first words on marriage: "For this cause a man shall leave his father and his mother, and shall cleave to his wife; and they shall become one flesh" (Gen. 2:24). In God's original blueprint for marriage in the Garden of Eden, husband and wife were to be glued together into one, inseparable unit. Period. Divorce wasn't even in the vocabulary.

God's Number One Plan

"So why did God allow Moses to include a divorce clause in the Old Testament law?" someone asks. "Because of your hardness of heart," Jesus replies (Mark 10:5). He meant that when sin entered the human race as described in Genesis 3, man became basically selfish, unloving and unforgiving in all his relationships—including marriage. The life of oneness God intended husband and wife to enjoy often resorted to a contest between two self-centered individuals. Instead of caring for each other selflessly, individuals care for themselves first. So for the man who was too hard-hearted to forgive his wife for burning the toast or for being unfaithful, God allowed divorce.

Does that mean that God scrapped His original blueprint of oneness for husband and wife when sin entered the picture? Not according to what Jesus said in Mark 10. After quoting Genesis 2:24 He added, "What therefore God has joined together, let no man separate" (Mark 10:9). God's number one plan for husband and wife is that they commit themselves to each other for keeps and work out the wrinkles of their relationship with selfless love and forgiveness.

Now let's talk about your divorce. "Wait a minute," you say, "I'm not even thinking about *marriage* yet, let alone divorce!" That's why *now* is the best time to talk about it. Otherwise you may also get vacuumed into the meet-fall-in-love-marry-fall-out-of-love-divorce cycle.

There is one key ingredient that can break the cycle and turn a marriage into the expression of oneness that God originally planned. That ingredient is glue. Genesis 2:24 literally commands a man to leave his parents and be glued to his wife. That's what the word "cleave" means.

Spiritual Crazy Glue

Falling in love, meaning the emotional side of love, is not strong enough to glue people together. Feelings come and go even in the best of marriages. A good feeling of love is not a stable foundation upon which to build a solid marriage.

The only kind of glue that holds a marriage together is the glue of *commitment*. "Oh," you say, "you mean having a marriage ceremony." No! Signing a marriage certificate and saying "I do" to a minister are part of it, but commitment is much deeper than that. Commitment means that you give yourself to your partner in marriage as a permanent gift; and the two of you give yourselves to God as one. This kind of glue bonds people together so that they can endure all the pressing, pulling, stretching, and twisting that life can inflict on them. Unless a man and woman are glued together by their commitment to each other, in the sight of God, all the romantic feelings in the world cannot keep their marriage secure in the complex maze of modern life.

Someday your prince or princess will probably come. You'll see pink hearts exploding in the sky, hear guitars when he/she speaks, and swear that you're in heaven whenever you're with that special person. That's called falling in love, and it's a beautiful experience. But trying to build a marriage on that feeling alone is like trying to bind two bricks together with cellophane tape; it will never stand the test of time.

Because the indestructible cement of commitment is needed to weld two people together in marriage, every person in love, before he or she says "I do," needs to wait until the hearts and guitars diminish long enough to hear himself/herself answer the question, "Am I ready to glue myself to this person for keeps?"

Carol and I have been "glued" for 15 years. The romance that bloomed in our late teens has developed into a lovely bouquet of deep caring for each other. The hearts and guitars are still present, but they are subservient to the glue of commitment that keeps us as close as two people can possibly be to each other.

I hope every one reading these pages falls in love. But I pray that you will cover the marriage partner you choose with the glue of your commitment to

him/her. If I may respectfully paraphrase Jesus'
words, "What God has glued together, man won't
want to separate by divorce."

SCENE 26: If I Were a Rich Man

Read Mark 10:17-31

The story is told of a multimillionaire who owned
nearly the entire city in which he lived. One day the
man died of a heart attack, and the population
mourned his loss. When his will was read, the man's
relatives discovered that he had some unusual instructions for his own funeral. The man requested
that his body be dressed in his most expensive clothes
and propped upright in the back seat of his solid gold
Cadillac convertible. The Cadillac was to be chauf-
feur-driven down Main Street to the cemetery while
flowers were strewn on the highway and marching
bands played the millionaire's favorite songs.

The day for the funeral arrived and all arrange-
ments for the procession were precisely followed.
Thousands of people lined Main Street to see the
event.

Meanwhile, a raggedy-looking hobo who had just
wandered into town saw the huge crowd and drew
closer to see what was going on. He watched amazed
as young girls marched down the street sprinkling
thousands of flowers on the pavement. He pressed in

closer to the crowd to see and hear the bands play the most beautiful music he had ever heard.

Then he saw the Cadillac in the distance. His eyes bulged with disbelief as he watched the sparkling limousine pass with the millionaire's corpse propped majestically in the back seat. The hobo was so overcome with awe that he could contain his silence no longer. He shouted out excitedly, "Now that's what I call really living!"

Most of us are a lot like that hobo. When we see a wallet that is fat with greenbacks we think, "Wow, what I could do with a wad of cash like that!" And when we see people loaded down with the treasures that money can buy—motorcycles, racy cars, expensive clothes—we sometimes find ourselves drooling with envy.

"Money isn't everything," we say jokingly, "but it's way ahead of whatever is in second place!" None of us would be disappointed if we found $10 in the street, won $5,000 on a TV game show or inherited half a million from a long-lost, departed uncle.

But we're like the hobo in another way. The hobo was dead wrong in his appraisal of the dead man's situation. What he thought was "really living" was only a funeral procession for a dead millionaire. Oftentimes we look at wealth, the people who have it, and the things it can buy and say, "Now that's really living!" But like the hobo, we don't always see the whole picture.

One Thing You Lack

In Mark 10:17-31, Jesus used a conversation with a rich young man to emphasize to His disciples, and to us, the disappointments and dangers of making wealth a primary goal in life. The young man seemed to have a serious interest in living a God-pleasing life. But Jesus was aware of one area in which the man had placed something else ahead of God. "And looking at him, Jesus felt a love for him, and said to him, 'One thing you lack: go and sell all you possess, and give it to the poor, and you shall have treasure in heaven; and come, follow Me' " (Mark 10:21).

Pow! Jesus' words scored a direct hit on the young man's wallet! The Master's command uncovered the "one thing" standing in the way of the young man's relationship to God—his desire for wealth. He was so attached to his possessions that he was unwilling to accept Jesus' offer of heavenly treasure and membership among His followers.

As the rich man walked sadly away, Jesus taught His disciples about the problems of wealth. "How hard it will be for those who are wealthy to enter the kingdom of God!... It is easier for a camel to go through the eye of a needle than for a rich man to enter the kingdom of God" (Mark 10:23,25).

"Who Needs God?"

Why is wealth such an obstacle to spiritual life and health? Because wealth is the most sinister counterfeit for God that man has ever devised. Let's face it. Wealth can solve problems, bring happiness and fulfill our material wants and needs. A person can become so reliant on wealth that he begins to wonder, "Who needs God?" No wonder Jesus said "No one can serve two masters; for either he will hate the one and love the other, or he will hold to the one and despise the other. You cannot serve God and Mammon [riches]" (Matt. 6:24).

Jesus did not say it's a sin to be rich; He said it is difficult to be rich and Christian at the same time because of the temptation to rely on wealth rather than God. He did not say it is wrong to want nice things; He said it is wrong to make things your major goal in life because first place is reserved for God.

Steve and Nolan, both juniors in high school, took jobs as box-boys in the same market. Steve's goal was to make as much money as possible so he could buy a car and enjoy a fun-filled social life before going away to college.

Nolan's goal was to have enough money for school expenses and some social activities, but his faithfulness to his church and his scholastic preparation for college were more important to him than his job.

Steve and Nolan were very good workers. So both were asked to work Sunday, 3:00 P.M. to midnight. Steve accepted because it meant a fatter paycheck. Nolan declined because he wanted to be involved in his Sunday evening youth group at church and because he felt that the late hour would rob him of needed rest for Monday.

By the end of his senior year, Steve had reached his goal. He drove one of the nicest cars in school and he could afford to date two or three nights a week. But in the process of reaching his goal Steve's church life and school life deteriorated. In the fall Steve had neither the grades nor the savings to start college. His busy social schedule had also crowded all church activities out of his life.

Nolan also reached his goal by graduation. He

hadn't earned as much money as Steve, but he finished high school with a 3.5 grade point average and received a scholarship for college. He had served as president of his youth group and watched it grow. Because of his faithful service to the youth group, his church awarded him with a dependable used car. In addition they promised prayer and financial support for his years in college.

Who's First?

Jesus' warning regarding wealth applies as much to Steve and Nolan as to the rich young man in Mark 10. And since you and I are not much different from Steve and Nolan, Jesus' words speak to us too. First place in our lives is not big enough to handle both God and the desire for riches. One of them must go. But we have the assurance from God that when we make the commitment to give Him top billing over our paychecks, allowances and savings accounts, He will actively meet our needs and throw in the bonus of "treasure in heaven" (Mark 10:21).

SCENE 27: Giving Your Way to Greatness

Read Mark 10:32-45

Once as a boy I mailed away for a nifty-looking moon village that was advertised on the back of a cereal box. The offer included rockets, space ports, living quarters for the astronauts and space flight centers. And the price was right: 75¢ and two box tops would bring me enough toys to fill an entire living room.

When the package finally came in the mail I was destroyed with disappointment. The moon village turned out to be several sheets of paper with the pieces of the village printed on them. A long list of detailed instructions explained how to cut, fold and tape together a very tiny and flimsy moon village. The real thing wasn't anything like what I had imagined from the artist's drawing on the cereal box.

As Jesus was leading His disciples toward Jerusalem, two of the disciples—James and John, the sons of Zebedee, let their imaginations run away with them. Jesus clearly stated—for the third time—the destiny awaiting Him at Jerusalem: "Behold, we are going up to Jerusalem, and the Son of Man will be delivered up to the chief priests and the scribes; and they will condemn Him to death, and will deliver Him up to the Gentiles. And they will mock Him and spit upon Him, and scourge Him, and kill Him, and three days later He will rise again" (Mark 10:33,34).

But James and John had stars in their eyes. They were imagining an entirely different conclusion to the journey—a revolution in which Jesus would overthrow, with supernatural power, the Roman military establishment in Jerusalem. In their minds, Jesus and His followers would soon rule Palestine.

The Zebedee brothers were so confident in their fantasy that they decided to apply early for two top cabinet positions. "Grant that we may sit in Your glory, one on Your right, and one on Your left"

(Mark 10:37). They were completely blind to Jesus' prediction of His coming suffering.

"Are you ready to go through everything I go through?" Jesus quizzed the two. He was thinking of the pain and humiliation of the trial, His beating and crucifixion. "Oh yes," they replied confidently. They were probably thinking of the excitement, adventure and glory of the revolution they expected in Jerusalem. Jesus looked ahead through the coming years and said, "The cup that I drink you shall drink; and you shall be baptized with the baptism with which I am baptized" (Mark 10:39). The Zebedee brothers may have thought that Jesus was granting their request for status in the revolutionary government they imagined. But the Master was referring to the fact that James would be rejected and killed (see Acts 12:2) and John would be rejected and exiled (see Rev. 1:9). Each would taste of the suffering that Jesus would soon experience in Jerusalem.

There are some Christians today who, like James and John, have a distorted picture of what it means to be a follower of Jesus. "What am I going to *gain* from being a Christian?" they ask. Jerry, an eleventh grader, thinks this way. As long as his parents are pleased with him and he has plenty of friends, Jerry finds it easy to be a Christian. But when his parents ground him for staying out too late or some of his friends snub him because he's involved in church, Jerry isn't so sure he wants to be a follower of Christ. "After all," Jerry thinks, "if God can't take care of these problems, what good is a Christianity?"

Many of us, like Jerry, James and John, have a hard

time getting the message; the Christian life is not a smooth-sailing, hassle-free, magic-carpet ride to heaven. We don't get to live the life of a king—at least not here on earth. We live the life of a servant!

Jesus said, "Whoever wishes to become great among you shall be your servant; . . . for even the Son of Man did not come to be served, but to serve, and to give His life a ransom for many" (Mark 10:43,45). Therefore, don't ask what you can *gain* from being a Christian (although the Bible assures us that the rewards and blessings of following Christ are endless). Rather, ask, "What can I give—as a servant of God, and of people?"

James and John became great, not by being prime ministers in the government of a political revolutionary, but by serving Christ and His church. Though they were far from understanding the path to greatness in Mark 10, they eventually realized that *giving*, not *getting*, is the heart of the Christian life.

The pattern for greatness among God's children is still the same.

SCENE 28: A Mission of Mercy

Read Mark 10:46-62

The president of the Jericho Chamber of Commerce was concluding his enthusiastic speech at the city gate. City dignitaries, Jesus of Nazareth, and a throng of people listened as they jostled one another through the gate on the road to Jerusalem.

"And so, we want to express our thanks to you, Jesus of Nazareth, for your brief visit—" A commotion behind the crowd interrupted the speaker.

"Jesus, Son of David, have mercy on me!" cried a muffled voice.

"Shut up, you blind fool," one of the dignitaries growled over his shoulder.

The Chamber president looked at Jesus nervously and continued. "We want to thank—"

"Jesus, Son of David, have mercy on me!" This time the voice from outside the circle was loud and demanding.

"Hush! Be quiet! Be still, old beggar!" several people joined in harshly.

But Jesus was visibly moved by what He heard from behind the pressing crowd. He called the blind beggar named Bartimaeus forward and asked him what he wanted. "My master, I want to regain my sight!" Bartimaeus begged Jesus eagerly.

"Your faith has made you well," Jesus replied. And immediately the blind beggar could see.

The Magic Word
What caused Jesus to turn His attention away from the large crowd to Bartimaeus, the rudely persistent, blind beggar and outcast? I think Jesus heard the word *mercy*, "Jesus, Son of David, have mercy on me!" (Mark 10:47,48).

What Is Mercy?
Mercy is compassion or pity that leads a person to

provide relief for someone in misery. A merciful person is one who feels deeply the hurts of others and acts to comfort and relieve those hurts. Agencies such as the Red Cross exercise mercy in an organized fashion. But you also show mercy in simple acts such as consoling and bandaging a little brother or sister who has skinned a knee.

Mercy is a primary ingredient in God's nature. The Lord said of Himself, "I am Jehovah, the merciful and gracious God" (Exod. 34:6, *TLB*). And Moses said, "The Lord your God is merciful" (Deut. 4:31, *TLB*).

Since Jesus was God in a human body, mercy was one of the essential characteristics of His earthly ministry. His heart of mercy was moved by the suffering of people, and His power, as God, allowed Him to exercise His mercy through His ministry of healing and deliverance.

My Master

You get the idea from Mark's report about Bartimaeus that the blind beggar could "see" much more than most people thought. First, he had heard enough about Jesus to correctly identify Him as "the Son of David" a title that designated Jesus as the promised Messiah—God come to earth.

Second, Bartimaeus knew enough about the God of his ancestors to know that the quality of mercy abounded in Him. He knew that God responded to the cry of one who suffered.

And third, Bartimaeus had faith to believe that Jesus was personally interested in him and would heal him. The word "Master" in verse 51 is *Rabboni*, and is a personal term meaning, "*my* master."

Jesus heard Bartimaeus cry for mercy and handed the blind beggar a blank check by saying, "What do you want Me to do for you?" Jesus Christ was merciful and willing to act compassionately to the faithful Bartimaeus. The result of the mission of mercy was a miracle.

Jesus *was* merciful and *is* merciful. The same quality of mercy that God evidenced in the Old Testament and Jesus demonstrated in the New Testament is available to anyone who sees Jesus through the eyes of faith as Bartimaeus did. Jesus knows where we're hurting and, when we turn to Him with our hurts, He is ready to say, "What do you want me to do for you?"

When Ben tore up his knee in the first game of the season he lost his chance for all-league honors. Jesus was aware of Ben's physical pain and his deep disappointment. When Julie blew an exam because she studied the wrong chapter, Jesus felt it. When Tanya's mother died of cancer, the same Jesus who was moved to compassion for Bartimaeus understood Tanya's grief.

There is no pain, disappointment, confusion, fear, or loneliness that Jesus cannot understand. And when you come to Him crying, "My Master, I need help," Christ responds with His ministry of compassion. Sometimes you see Him when He supernaturally restores someone's health. Other times you see Him through the caring of a concerned Christian friend who prays for you in time of trouble.

Bartimaeus could have felt that he was not very important in God's sight. He was only a useless, blind beggar, a social outcast. But because he approached Christ with confidence, he discovered that he was of supreme importance to God. The Master met his need.

You may feel that you don't have a special place in God's plans. You may feel that your hurts are not important to God because you're so insignificant. You may believe that God doesn't have time to bother with you. But if God's mercy can reach poor Bartimaeus, think what He has waiting for *you* when you call on Him.

SCENE 29: Following the Game Plan

Read Mark 11:1-11

In the midst of the pro football season one year, the Los Angeles Rams registered a big win that kept them in contention for the divisional championship. In a newspaper interview the following day, the Rams' quarterback stated that one of his team's touchdowns came about in an unusual way.

It seems that one of the offensive guards kept insisting that the quarterback call a certain play. "I resisted the suggestion," stated the quarterback, "because the play was not in our game plan for that day." (For you non-fans, a game plan is a specific assortment of plays a team decides to employ based on particular objectives they have for that game.)

Finally, the quarterback gave in to his guard's persistence and called the play. The result was a 40-yard touchdown gallop. The quarterback closed the interview by quipping, "If that's how his [the guard's] ideas are going to work, I'll let him call every play!"

In a sense, Jesus was following a game plan during His earthly ministry. God the Father and Jesus the Son planned the Saviour's visit to planet earth before the world was created. When Jesus inserted Himself into human history as a baby in Bethlehem, His life's work and destiny had already been established. And He was totally committed to that game plan. As an adult Jesus boldly stated, "My food is to do the will of Him who sent Me, and to accomplish His work" (John 4:34). Jesus had been equipped with a game plan (God's will). And with every word, act and step Jesus demonstrated His willingness to follow the game plan to the letter.

In a football game, a team does not want to broadcast its game plan to its opponent. Obviously, if the other team knew what you were planning to do, they would know how to stop you. But in the case of Jesus and His game plan, God broadcast many key elements of the game plan to the world ahead of time so that people would be ready to receive the Saviour when He arrived.

We refer to God's pre-broadcast as "prophecy." Most of the key events of Jesus' life and ministry were carefully recorded in the Old Testament centuries before Jesus was born. Over 300 specific prophecies about Jesus are found in the prophetic writings of the Old Testament—prophecies concerning the place of His birth (Mic. 5:2), the virginity of His mother (Isa. 7:14), the place of His ministry (Isa. 9:1,2), His rejection (Isa. 53:3), death (Isa. 53:12) and resurrection (Ps. 16:10).

The Game Plan

Mark 11:1-11 describes the beginning of the most agonizing week of Jesus Christ's game plan. It was the week of rejection, suffering and death that Jesus had told His disciples about so openly. Ironically, the week began with an event that looked anything like the beginning of a week of suffering—Jesus' triumphant ride into Jerusalem.

Jesus' entrance into Jerusalem on a donkey was another event in the game plan that God previewed for the world in Old Testament Scriptures. The prophet Zechariah wrote, "Rejoice greatly, O daughter of Zion! Shout in triumph, O daughter of Jerusalem! Behold your king is coming to you; He is just and endowed with salvation, humble, and mounted on a donkey, even on a colt, the foal of a donkey" (Zech. 9:9). God's game plan called for the Messiah to enter Jerusalem in the humble simplicity of a servant, so He rode a donkey's colt. The fact that Jesus called for a colt "on which no one yet has ever sat" (Mark 11:2) was also significant to the plan. In Jewish tradition, an unbroken animal was often associated with sacred use.

Even though the game plan called for Jesus to enter Jerusalem as a servant, the people saw Him as a political saviour who would oust the Roman tyrants governing their holy city. The people cried out, "Hosanna!" (Mark 11:9) which meant, "Save us now, we pray!" It was a plea for political liberation.

The people also shouted, "Blessed is He who comes in the name of the Lord" (Mark 11:9). Along with the hosannas, this line was often chanted by pilgrims entering Jerusalem and by priests as part of the Hebrew worship liturgy. The people imagined that Jesus would use His miracle-working power to fulfill their prayer for political salvation. They wanted a liberator on a white charger, but God's game plan called for a servant on a lowly donkey.

The Team

Notice how Jesus used two of His disciples in carrying out this portion of the game plan. "Go . . . find a colt . . . untie it and bring it here" (Mark 11:2). The disciples could have said, "What if we don't find a colt and, if we do, what if we get arrested for taking it?" But the disciples trusted Jesus enough to follow His instructions. As a result they became partners with Jesus Christ in the execution of the game plan.

The focus of God's game plan is redemption. Jesus Christ paid the death penalty for our sin in order to redeem us for God. However, even though God's game plan was completed with the death and resurrection of Christ (see John 17:4; 19:30), the play continues. For the redemption that Christ secured for all people must be accepted individually by each person. "The Lord is . . . not willing that any should perish, but that all should come to repentance" (2 Pet. 3:9, *KJV*). So as long as there are those who have not accepted the redemption of Christ, God's game plan continues.

Just as Jesus used two disciples to carry out His game plan in Mark 11, so He uses people today to carry out the game plan of redemption. He still looks for willing followers who will obey His instructions trustfully like the disciples who "went away and found a colt . . . and they untied it . . . .And they brought the colt to Jesus" (Mark 11:4,7).

When Becky and Sherrie gave their testimonies at a church youth outreach rally, they were participating in God's game plan of redemption by sharing the good news with others. When Margaret and a group of her friends took part in a missionary venture to Baja California over Thanksgiving vacation, they also were cooperating with the game plan. Wherever individuals are serving Christ with their lives and reaching out to others, God's game plan is being executed.

As a Christian, you are already in the game. Giving your life to Christ made you a member of God's team. The question is, are you actively participating in the game plan, or just sitting on the bench sipping Gatorade?

SCENE 30: Here Comes the Judge

Read Mark 11:12-26

I'll never forget an afternoon I spent in court with my friend Sherm. Sherm had been arrested for drunk driving and was ordered to appear in municipal court for a disposition of his case by the presiding judge.

The judge before whom Sherm was to stand was known to be very hard on drunk driving offenders. Sherm was understandably nervous as I drove him to court. He was expecting a heavy fine, jail sentence and/or suspension of his driver's license.

The courtroom was crowded that day with other drunk driving offenders and their sympathetic friends and relatives. One by one, the judge called them to the bench. Most of them pleaded guilty. When they did, the judge quizzed them about their offense and lectured them sternly for violating the law and, in the process, endangering the lives of other citizens. Most of the defendants walked sadly away from the bench having received fines, brief jail sentences and suspension of driving privileges. Sherm trembled at my side as he waited for his name to be called.

Finally my friend was summoned forward. The judge quietly reviewed the charges and then asked Sherm for his plea. Sherm confessed his guilt and then, in quavering voice, explained that he had already sought out counseling for his drinking problem. Sherm hoped that his attempts at rehabilitation would encourage the judge to soften his sentence.

Again the judge launched into a stern reprimand and scolded Sherm for the seriousness of his offense. Then he sentenced Sherm to a suspended jail term, levied a fine of several hundred dollars and suspended his driver's license for one year.

Sherm walked out of court that day grateful that he did not have to go to jail but sobered by the experience of his appearance before the bench. I went away thinking about the judge. He was a man who probably played golf with his associates, socialized with his friends and wrestled with his children just like any other man. But when he donned his black robe and took his seat behind the bench, he was a man consumed with obedience to the law, and he made life miserable for lawbreakers who stepped before him for judgment.

The Fig Tree

In Mark 11:12-26, Mark sketches two quick portraits of Jesus Christ in a role we sometimes fail to see. These verses do not show the meek and mild Jesus of our childhood stories. Rather we see Jesus Christ the judge—standing firm against unrighteousness and executing judgment on offenders of God's law.

The first incident shows Jesus coming to a fig tree with the intention of picking and eating some fruit from it. However, the tree had leaves but no fruit. Seeing this, Jesus uttered a statement of judgment as His disciples listened: "May no one ever eat fruit from you again!" (Mark 11:14). When Jesus and the disciples passed by the fig tree the next day it was completely withered.

Most scholars see the fig tree cursing as an object lesson parable. The fig tree represents Israel, barren because her devotion to God had grown cold by Jesus' day. The curse in verse 14 meant that Israel, the nation through which God intended to bless the world, was about to be set aside because she had rejected Jesus as her Messiah.

The Desecrators

The second sketch shows Jesus in the Temple area

111

expelling those who were desecrating the "house of prayer" (Mark 11:17). There were at least five types of offenders according to Mark's report. The first two were "those who were buying and selling in the temple." The charge compared the Temple to a noisy marketplace where merchants hawked a variety of items used in Temple worship.

Then there were "the moneychangers," those who exchanged foreign coins of visiting Jews for Jewish shekels so that male Jews could pay their annual Temple tax. (The moneychangers tagged on about a 15 percent charge for their services.)

"Those who were selling doves" had a supply of birds on hand for anyone who came to make sacrifice but did not have an animal to use.

Finally, there were those who would "carry goods through the temple" (Mark 11:16). These were people who were taking a short-cut through the Temple area in the process of carrying on their daily business.

It is generally thought that all this activity was taking place in a Temple area known as the court of the Gentiles. Since Gentiles (non-Jews) were not allowed inside the Temple proper, the only place available to them for prayer and worship was the outer court of the Gentiles. But the racket of buyers and sellers haggling over prices, coins changing hands, birds squawking and merchants passing through made the atmosphere anything but worshipful.

Jesus the judge saw the sacrilege and injustice with which the people had polluted the Temple, and He executed judgment on them. In what must have been an impressive display of authority, Jesus sent merchants scurrying, coins rolling and birds flying as He cleared the courtyard of the distractions to prayer.

This is a facet of Jesus that we don't look at very closely. Youthful Christians particularly like to see Jesus as our bosom-buddy who understands our slang, laughs at our jokes and overlooks our pranks.

Sure, Jesus is our friend. But He is also a righteous and loving judge. He's not just looking for buddies to pal around with, but men and women who will live lives of righteousness. As Peter expressed it, "God is not one to show partiality, but in every nation the man who fears Him and does what is right, is welcome to Him" (Acts 10:34,35).

Friend and judge—yes, Jesus is both. He is the perfect blend of love and justice. His love forgives our sins but His justice confronts us with the task of clearing sin out of our lives and replacing it with righteousness.

Friend and judge, love and justice. You can't have one without the other.

SCENE 31: Loaded Questions

Read Mark 11:27—12:37

"We must annihilate Him," the Pharisee breathed venomously near the ear of the scribe as they watched Jesus gratify the people with His masterful teaching.

"You've been saying that for months, righteous one," replied the scribe. "But what is your plan? The Nazarene continues to hold the attention of our people. They no longer listen to us interpret the law to them; they desire only to hear His words about love and submit to the sorcery He calls healing."

"I still think we should ambush Him on the road to Bethany some night, kill Him and throw His body down a dry well," the Pharisee whispered.

"The people, righteous one, are too many. They surround Him every hour. They are as loyal to Him as our fathers were to the prophets."

"How then?" the Pharisee demanded angrily.

"We can do nothing until we set the people against Him," answered the scribe. "We must get Him to say something that displeases the people. We must hang Him on His own words with loaded questions. Questions that will anger some people no matter how He answers."

This conversation is not in the Bible, but it probably typifies the frustration Jewish religious leaders felt as they watched Jesus win the allegiance of the crowds away from their teaching. The leaders would have abducted Him and murdered Him except they feared the reprisal of the crowd. So they resorted to trick questions attempting to tangle Jesus in His words and thus discredit Him with some faction of the crowd.

In this scene, Mark records several loaded questions the religious leaders asked Jesus in their drive to find a weakness in His theology. Three of the questions exploded in the faces of the pompous chief priests, scribes and elders. And one was salvaged and recycled by Jesus to minister to a leader who had a deeper interest than to undermine the rabbi from Nazareth.

Authority

The first question was, "By what authority are You doing these things, or who gave You this authority to do these things?" (Mark 11:28). The question was asked by a representative group from the Sanhedrin, which was the council of religious authority for the Jews. In their question they were saying, "We didn't give you authority to teach the people, so who do you think you are?"

Jesus threw the question right back at them by quizzing them on the authority of John the Baptist. "Was the baptism of John from heaven, or from men?" (Mark 11:30). John the Baptist hadn't been authorized by the Sanhedrin either, but he sparked a genuine revival in Palestine that turned multitudes of people to God.

Mark 11:31,32 gives us a peek inside the leaders' huddle and reveals the dilemma Jesus' question caused for them. Their question had not trapped Jesus, but His question trapped them! "We can't say," stammered the leaders defensively. "Neither can I," replied Jesus.

The source of authority for John's and Jesus' ministry was obvious to everyone watching except the hard-nosed religious leaders. God was their authority. Jesus added the parable of the vine-growers to underscore His unspoken answer regarding His authority as the Son of God.

End of round one. Score: Jesus--1, enemies--0.

Taxes

The second question of this set was, "Is it lawful to pay a poll-tax to Caesar, or not?" It was posed by representatives of the Pharisees and Herodians. The Pharisees were legalistic supporters of the law and national freedom, and against support of Rome. The Herodians were Jews who supported Herod in his submission to Rome and favored paying taxes to Caesar. The two groups were mortal enemies, but here they were united in their attempt to trap Jesus. If Jesus answered "pay," He was in trouble with the Pharisees. If He answered "don't pay," He was in trouble with the Herodians. The trap was set.

Again the loaded question misfired. "Render to Caesar the things that are Caesar's," Jesus replied, "and to God the things that are God's" (Mark 12:17). The answer scorched both the Pharisees and Herodians. The Pharisees needed to know that those things that were stamped with Caesar's image, like coins, belonged to Caesar. It was right for them to pay taxes to support the government that provided them "good social order, economic stability (even if the sales and food taxes ran high) and worldwide peace, the *pax romana.*"[1]

And the Herodians needed to know that those things that were stamped with God's image, namely their hearts, belonged to God. They were not to worship Caesar as the Romans did, but God, to whom they belonged.

End of round two. Score: Jesus–2, enemies–0.

Eternal Life

Question 3 was posed by the Sadducees, a small

but powerful sect of Jews who accepted only the first five books of the Old Testament. The Sadducees refused to believe in the resurrection and eternal life. Their loaded question focused on an absurd story they felt proved their point that there would be no afterlife. During the course of her life, the story went, a woman outlived seven successive husbands. "In the resurrection ..." asked the Sadducees tongue-in-cheek, "which one's wife will she be?" (Mark 12:23). They felt that the confusion inherent in their hypothetical situation proved their point.

Jesus defused the Sadducees' loaded question with a loaded statement. He said, "You do not understand the Scriptures, or the power of God" (Mark 12:24). The Sadducees' problem was that they were lousy Bible students. As a result, they were spiritually impotent. Not only had they limited God's Word to the Torah (Genesis, Exodus, Leviticus, Numbers and Deuteronomy), but they had also neglected to study even the little they accepted. Consequently Jesus deflated the crafty Sadducees with a quote from the Torah which proved that there is life after death: "Have you not read ... 'I am the God of Abraham, and the God of Isaac, and the God of Jacob'? He is not the God of the dead, but of the living; you are greatly mistaken" (Mark 12:26,27, quoting Exod. 3:6).

End of round three. Score: Jesus–3, enemies–0.

Foremost Commandment

Question 4 in this scene has a slightly different complexion to it. Mark's report suggests that the man asking the question, although it may have been an-

117

other loaded question, was sincerely interested in Jesus' response.

The question was a common one to the Pharisees: "What commandment is the foremost of all?" The Pharisees had added so many nit-picking rules to God's law that they were always being asked, "What is the law in a nutshell?" A common Gentile challenge to the Jews was, "I'll become a convert to Judaism if you can teach me the whole law while I stand on one foot."

Jesus summarized every commandment in all the books of the Bible when He answered, "The foremost is, 'Hear, O Israel; The Lord our God is one Lord; and you shall love the Lord your God with all your heart, and with all your soul, and with all your mind, and with all your strength.' The second is this, 'You shall love your neighbor as yourself.' There is no other commandment greater than these" (Mark 12:29-31 quoting Deut. 6:4,5 and Lev. 19:18). God's message to man in a nutshell is, "Love God and love people."

The questioning scribe lit up in agreement. "This is what I believe also," the man was saying in Mark 13:32,33. "Loving God and one's neighbor is more important than the sacrifices and burnt offerings we prize so highly."

Jesus' reply to the scribe, "You are not far from the kingdom of God" (Mark 12:34), indicates that although the answer was correct, there was something missing in what the young man said. Apparently Jesus was saying, "Your answer is right. All you need to do is start putting it into practice. Loving God and loving people is not just head knowledge—it's action."

End of round four. Final score: Jesus–4, enemies–0. "And after that, no one would venture to ask Him any more questions" (Mark 12:34).

Jesus' enemies were unsuccessful in their attempt to lead Him into self-incriminating statements. He successfully turned their verbal missiles into opportunities to declare God's truth.

Verbal abuse and loaded questions are still being thrown at Jesus' followers today in an attempt to discredit their faith before others. Rita took a lot of flack from her biology class when she gave a report favoring the creationist view of the origin of man. During a debate on capital punishment, Woody's argument was rejected because he used the Bible to support his view.

Two key resources are at your disposal if you are a believer that will help you defuse loaded questions and arguments. First, you have the model of Jesus Christ in Mark 11:27—12:37 and other Scriptures. By watching how Jesus handled His enemies' assaults, you know better how to respond when you're under similar fire.

Second, you have the Holy Spirit within you to help you make the right responses. This is the same resource Jesus relied upon, and He is available to us today! Great news!

None of us are anxious for the verbal potshots others take at us, but Christ has given us plenty of ammunition for returning the fire in a way that will silence critics, and eventually win some of them.

Note

1. Ralph P. Martin, *Where the Action Is* (Glendale, Calif.: Regal Books, 1977), p. 104.

SCENE 32: Give Till It Hurts

Read Mark 12:38-44

When my family and I first met Esther Pillon she was in her late fifties, single and living alone in a small house in our little town. She was so painfully shy in public that she was often overlooked in a crowd. She was the kind of person who was content to blend in with the wallpaper and not be noticed.

I was Esther Pillon's pastor for two and a half years. She was one among the faithful few who rarely missed a church service. But I'll remember her best for her generosity. Whenever my wife, children or I had a birthday, Esther quietly presented us with a birthday card. Inside, in addition to kind words of blessing and thankfulness, each of us would find a monetary gift. The kids would receive two or three dollars, and Carol and I would find ten to twenty dollars in our birthday cards.

When our family went on vacation, Esther would slip us a few dollars for spending money. On other occasions she would give a card or a gift—always in her shy, unpretentious way.

We moved away from that little town and lost touch with most of the parishioners including Esther Pillon. A few years later we learned that Esther had become ill and died. Then came some amazing news. We learned that Esther Pillon had been living on a total of about $150 per month—less than if she had been on welfare! One of the most generous persons I have ever known, and yet she barely had enough to keep herself supplied with necessities of life. But she gave generously to others as if she were wealthy.

One day Jesus went into the treasury of the Temple and saw a woman who, like Esther Pillon, was a sacrificial giver. The treasury was a certain section or room in the Temple where the Jews brought the various offerings the law prescribed. The treasury contained 13 horn-shaped receptacles, each one to receive a different offering—for the Temple, for the priests, for the poor, etc.

When a contributor came to the treasury, he was required to state the amount of his donation and the designation of his offering. Naturally, when some of the big spenders stepped into the treasury they made sure everyone heard how many bags of silver were being dropped into the coffers. It was a great chance to score points publicly as a big-hearted philanthropist.

When Jesus "sat down opposite the treasury, and began observing how the multitude were putting money into the treasury" (Mark 12:41), He was looking with a discerning eye at the motives that brought people to the offering horns. He watched the wealthy givers proudly announce their substantial gifts as the commoners oohed and ahhed, and the Temple officers applauded.

But then "a poor widow came and put in two small copper coins" (Mark 12:42). The coins mentioned were the smallest in circulation and represented the smallest offering the law allowed. Perhaps the disciples were chuckling about her apparently insignificant contribution.

But Jesus, after watching the incident with pure eyes, called His disciples into a quick conference. "Truly I say to you, this poor widow put in more than all the contributors to the treasury" (Mark 12:43). The disciples must have looked at each other questioningly. "Was He looking at the same woman we were looking at? She only put in two copper coins while J. Sylvester Moneybags over there dropped in a cool thousand."

But Jesus continued: "For they all put in out of their surplus, but she, out of her poverty, put in all she owned, all she had to live on" (Mark 12:44). Aha! Jesus wasn't looking at totals, He was looking at percentages. It's not how much you give that counts, it's how much you give compared to how much you *could* give. J. Sylvester Moneybags' offering was little more than pocket change in comparison to his huge bank account. But the widow gave everything she had, possibly depriving herself and family of a meal or two. Now that's giving till it hurts!

The Open-Hand Policy

In my study of the New Testament, I find one overriding principle about giving. It's not the tithe, although that's a good place to start. (The tithe means ten percent). It's not even a double tithe. Everywhere I look I see the open-hand policy. Luke says it this way, "If you give, you will get! Your gift will return to you in full and overflowing measure, pressed down, shaken together to make room for more, and running over. Whatever measure you use to give— large or small—will be used to measure what is given back to you" (Luke 6:38, *TLB*).

122

Simply, the open-hand policy means first that the believer's hands are open to give whatever he has to whoever needs it. A friend leaves his lunch at home so you open your brown bag and gladly share everything with him (even dessert!). A member of your Sunday School class is too broke to go to camp so you open your wallet and give him the seven bucks you were saving for spending money. A family at church lost all their possessions in a fire that destroyed their home so you give half your wardrobe to a girl in the family who is your size.

That's the open-hand policy. Give until the needs are met, or until there is nothing left to give.

But there is another side to the open-hand policy. That's the open-hand that is ready to receive what God is going to pour into it as a result of your giving. That's the "your gift will return to you in full and overflowing measure" part of Luke 6:38. God has promised if we give with abandon, so will He. "Oh good," you say, "I want to give more so I can get more!" Hey, that's not exactly how the open-hand policy is stated. Give without thought of return, and especially without planning on the return. Then it will be God's good pleasure to surprise you by pouring His gift into your open hands.

The poor widow was an open-handed giver; some of the rich people at the treasury, though their gifts were more substantial than the widow's, were not open-handed. It doesn't take a lot of money or possessions to be an open-handed giver. It just takes a little practice. Why not start this week by pulling a dollar out of your wallet or purse and asking God to show you a place where that dollar will be more useful than in your possession. You'll be amazed at how rewarding it can be to be an open-handed giver.

SCENE 33: Signs of the Times

Read Mark 13:1-37

Suppose you had the ability to see into the future. You could predict every gain and decline of the stock market, the winner of the Rose Bowl, the World Series and the Kentucky Derby. You could tell where oil, coal, gold and diamonds were waiting to be discovered. You would be so rich that there wouldn't be enough banks to hold all your money.

You would also be a world hero by predicting earthquakes, tornados, and other disasters in time to save the lives of millions. Your knowledge of the future would equip you to prevent wars, accidents and crime. But perhaps the greatest benefit of knowing the future would be that you would never get stuck on a blind date with someone you didn't like!

Coming back to reality, we know the future is a frontier that man with all his intelligence and technology has not been able to pry open. Everybody on our planet walks into the future together, one second at a time.

In Mark 13, Jesus made a statement about the destruction of the Temple that prompted a discussion of future events with four of His disciples. Peter,

James, John and Andrew asked Jesus, "Tell us, when will these things be, and what will be the sign when all these things are going to be fulfilled?" (Mark 13: 4). Jesus responded to the question by giving what is commonly called the Olivet discourse, a lecture on future events given on the Mount of Olives.

Looking at future events in the Bible is like looking at a series of mountain ranges through binoculars. The scene appears to be two dimensional with each range of mountains lying flat against the next. In reality there are often many miles between each range in our view.

Similarly, the future events in the Olivet discourse seem to lie flat against one another with no distinction of time between them. But Bible scholars generally believe that Jesus was referring to three specific time slots in the future: the early church; the fall of Jerusalem; the return of Christ. There are some elements from each of the three time slots that apply to Christians today. Let's keep our eyes open for these as we skim over the peaks of these three ranges.

The Early Church (Mark 13:5-13)

Jesus' message regarding future events for the early church centered on persecution. He looked ahead to the first few decades after His ascension and warned that the enemies of Christianity "will deliver you up to the courts, and you will be flogged in the synagogues, and you will stand before governors and kings for My sake, as a testimony against them" (Mark 13:9). The Master did not try to soft-pedal the life-style that awaited His followers any more than He tried to hide His own fate from them.

125

But He was also realistic about the resource that would be available to His followers in the midst of their persecution. Jesus encouraged them to relax and boldly voice their testimonies, "For it is not you who speak, but it is the Holy Spirit" (Mark 13:11). The Master brightened a discouraging prophecy by adding an encouraging promise.

Even though we are not members of that early church, Christians today are still sometimes hassled for their faith. But the same Holy Spirit resides within us so that we can "make a defense to every one who asks you to give an account for the hope that is in you" (1 Pet. 3:15).

The Fall of Jerusalem (Mark 13:14-20)

The second mountain peak in Jesus' future talk is generally thought to refer to an event that began in A.D. 66. A Jewish struggle for independence from Rome erupted which led to the utter destruction of Jerusalem and the annihilation of its inhabitants under the Roman general Vespasian and his son Titus in A.D. 70.

With this future event in view, Jesus warned the inhabitants of Jerusalem to head for the hills "when you see the abomination of desolation standing where it should not be" (Mark 13:14). Apparently the phrase "abomination of desolation" was familiar enough to the readers that Mark did not need to explain. It is thought to refer to an act of sacrilege committed in the Temple (such as a pig, unclean to the Jews, being sacrificed on the altar).

Ancient history tells us that many Jews did heed Jesus' warning and escaped to the elevated city of

Pella. But many more were slaughtered than were saved, and Jerusalem was left a smoldering heap of rubble.

The Return of Christ (Mark 13:21-37)

Jesus moved from the relatively near future to the third and most distant event when He began relating the wrap-up of world history as signaled by His return to earth. He mentioned two general indicators leading up to earth's final curtain: First, "False Christs and false prophets will arise, and will show signs and wonders, in order, if possible, to lead the elect astray" (Mark 13:22). Second, a series of celestial phenomena will take place involving the sun, moon and stars— "and the powers that are in the heavens will be shaken" (Mark 13:25).

Both of these indicators seem strangely up-to-date. Countless pseudo-Christian and anti-Christian religions and cults are reaching out to the unwary population. Mormonism, a cult based on the "revelation" of a nineteenth century false prophet named Joseph Smith, is flourishing. Eastern pantheistic religions still capture many people. And godless religions of the mind steer people away from faith in God to faith in their own intelligence as a priority.

Also, mankind's giant leap into space and his snowballing space technology have drawn our attention to the heavenly bodies that Jesus spoke about in His discourse. We don't know if the rearrangement of sun, moon and stars is literal or figurative. But reference to these elements is certainly a point of focus for outer space, science fiction-oriented humans.

The persecution of the early church and the fall of

Jerusalem are history. We have the advantage of reading Jesus' prophetic words in Mark 13 and their fulfillment in the records of history. But concerning Jesus' return at the end of the age we have only the clues He gave. "But of that day or hour no one knows . . . but the Father alone" (Mark 13:32).

But just as Jesus gave instructions to His disciples for handling the first two future events, so His words come to us as the third event approaches. "Be on the alert . . . lest he come suddenly and find you asleep" (Mark 13:35,36). In these words I hear Jesus saying, "Keep one eye on the signs of the times, but keep the other eye—and your hands and feet—busy serving Christ at home, on the campus, on the job and in the neighborhood."

SCENE 34: Money's No Object, King Jesus

Read Mark 14:1-11

Brother Sun, Sister Moon is a movie about the life of St. Francis of Assisi. The film follows St. Francis from his teen years as a soldier, through his conversion experience and into the priesthood.

As the son of a wealthy textile merchant, Francis is destined to inherit his father's business and live his life in comfort and ease as a successful businessman. But after his conversion Francis is uncomfortable with his wealth in the light of the poverty which abounded in Assisi. He feels that, since Christ gave up the treasures of heaven to become the Saviour, he must follow suit. One sequence from the film that is vivid in my memory shows Francis racing through his father's textile mill gathering bolts of colorful cloth and tossing them out the window to the city's poor who scrambled frantically to collect the windfall. From that time on St. Francis lived his life in poverty and gave himself to minister to the poor. St. Francis' response to his salvation involved renouncing his wealth and turning his money into a tribute to his newfound Saviour.

In Mark 14:1-11, Mark gives us a portrait of two individuals. One, like St. Francis, felt that money was no object in making tribute to Christ the King. The other had such a desire for money that it led him to perform the most dastardly deed in history.

An Act of Tribute

Two days before the Last Supper, a woman visited Jesus in the home of Simon the leper in Bethany. She brought "an alabaster vial of costly perfume of pure nard; and she broke the vial and poured it over His [Jesus'] head" while he was at the table (Mark 14:3). She was anointing Jesus in a way that was reminiscent of the anointing of Jewish kings in Old Testament times. The woman had keen insight into Christ's regal ancestry and quietly proclaimed Him her King with her loving deed.

"What a waste!" thought some of the disciples. "That perfume was worth a good share of an average man's yearly salary. If she would only have donated it to us intact instead of breaking it and using it all, we could have sold it and helped a lot of people."

The disciples' idea was not a bad one, but Jesus suggested that the woman's idea at that time was a better one. "She has done a good deed to Me" (Mark 14:6). There's a time for using money to help the underprivileged, and there's a time for using money specifically to make tribute to our Lord and King.

An Act of Betrayal

In contrast to the woman's act of submissive tribute to Jesus, Mark paints a dark picture of Judas Iscariot preparing to commit an act of betrayal against his Master. Whereas the woman gladly expended great wealth, possibly her life savings, in her tribute of perfume, and received Jesus' blessing, Judas' greed led to his downfall.

According to John's report, Judas was the one who led the grumbling about the woman's extravagant expense. Furthermore, John adds, "Not that he cared for the poor, but he was in charge of the disciples' funds and often dipped into them for his own use!" (John 12:6, *TLB*).

The chief priests, who wanted to do away with Jesus, recognized Judas' thirst for money so they "promised to give him money. And he began seeking how to betray Him at an opportune time" (Mark 14:11).

I'd like to be able to say to Jesus, "You are my King and money is no object in my desire to pay tribute to you." But too many times I have a touch of Judas in me that wants to glom onto the few coins I possess and use them for myself rather than honor my King with them.

130

Above and Beyond

I see tribute money as different from my regular tithe and offering-type giving. Tithes and offerings are gifts that I give regularly to the church and other organizations for the work of the church in my neighborhood and around the world. But a gift of tribute to Jesus as King is spontaneous, and above and beyond all I do as a regular church-giver. It's a special gift by which I say, "Jesus, I just want to say in this special way that you are my King and you're more important to me than whatever this money could buy me."

How do we pay tribute to Christ as King when He is not here in the flesh? One good way is to pay tribute in Christ's name to someone who *is* here in the flesh. Here are a few suggestions showing how you could honor Christ through someone else:

Buy your pastor or youth leader a gift—a shirt, tie, purse, necklace, etc.

Donate a certain amount of money to your favorite charity in recognition of Christ's lordship over you.

Fix your family a special dinner.

Make a special contribution to your church building fund, camping fund or other special project.

Find out what your best friend has always wanted and make every effort to buy it for him or her.

Tribute gifts such as these will be more meaningful to you if you give them anonymously. This will help you keep your focus on the real purpose of the gift— bringing tribute to Christ. He'll be the only one who knows "who dunnit"!

Mark does not record the name of the woman who honored Jesus in Bethany with the expensive perfume. But we do have her example. She has shown us how simple people, like you and me, can declare Christ's lordship in a practical, loving way with our possessions.

SCENE 35: Dinner in a Time Machine

Read Mark 14:12-26

"Look Peter, there he is!" John elbowed his fellow disciple in the ribs and pointed across the crowded street to a young man weaving through the bustling throng. He was carrying a clay pot that sloshed water over the rim with every step.

"I never thought I'd see the day: a man doing a woman's job of lugging water!" Peter chuckled.

"There's no doubt about it," John said with a smile, "that's the man the Master told us to follow." John tugged at Peter's shirtsleeve and the two of them merged with the crowd, their eyes glued to the man carrying the water pot.

Peter and John caught up with the young man just as he stepped through the gate into a large courtyard of a private home. "May we speak with your master, good sir?" John asked.

"You must be the men my father told me about," replied the young man as he lowered the water pot to the tile porch. "You *do* want to see the room we have prepared for your Passover feast, don't you?"

Peter and John exchanged glances of amazement. "Yes," replied Peter, "but how did you know?"

"Both my father and mother are followers of your Master," the young man answered as he dipped cups of water for his visitors. "Father knew that your Master would need a room for Passover. Well, it's ready. He knew you would come."

Just then an older gentleman appeared in the doorway, warmly greeted the disciples and escorted them to a spacious second-story room that overlooked the courtyard. "I think you'll find everything here you need—dishes, goblets, platters and linen," said the man. "It's ready and it's yours. All you need to prepare is the Passover meal."

The disciples thanked their gracious host, descended the stairs and crossed the courtyard toward the gate. "May God be with you," called the man from the second-story balcony, "and grant you and your Master a Passover feast you will long remember."

A Journey into the Past

The details and dialogue of the opening paragraphs are only speculative but, however it happened, the stage was set for the most meaningful Passover meal the disciples would ever experience.

In a sense, the Upper Room where Jesus gathered with His disciples that evening became a time machine. The Passover celebration was to be a journey into the distant past and prophetic voyage into the immediate and distant future.

As for the past, the Passover meal took its participants back about 1500 years in Israel's history. On the eve of Israel's deliverance from Egypt, God, through Moses, instructed every family to kill a lamb, sprinkle its blood on the doorposts of their home and gather inside for a meal of lamb, unleavened bread and bitter herbs.

Why such specific instructions? "For I will go through the land of Egypt on that night and will strike down all the first-born in the land of Egypt . . . . And the blood shall be a sign for you on the houses where you live; and when I see the blood I will pass over you, and no plague will befall you to destroy you when I strike the land of Egypt" (Exod. 12:12,13).

God dealt a death blow to godless Egypt and only those gathered inside a blood-marked home were safe.

Every year since that evening in Egypt the Jews have celebrated their deliverance from Egypt by eating the same Passover meal. "Now this day will be a memorial to you, and you shall celebrate it as a feast to the Lord; throughout your generations you are to celebrate it as a permanent ordinance" (Exod. 12:14). As Jesus and His disciples ate the Passover meal together their thoughts were carried back to Egypt to the God who delivered their ancestors from bondage.

A Journey into the Future

But the event we call the Last Supper was not only a journey into the past for Jesus' disciples, but a journey into the future as well. Jesus took unleavened bread from the Passover table, blessed it, broke it and looked ahead to His crucifixion when He said, "This is My body which is given for you" (Luke 22:19). Similarly, He took a cup of wine and said, "This is My blood of the covenant, which is to be shed on behalf of many" (Mark 14:24). Matthew adds the phrase, "for forgiveness of sins" (Matt. 26:28). The same Passover menu that pointed back to a sacrificial lamb and deliverance from Egypt also pointed forward to "the Lamb of God who takes away the sin of the world" (John 1:29).

Today, many Christians around the world participate regularly in a symbolic meal called the Lord's Supper, Holy Communion, the Eucharist, the Love Feast, or other designation. Some do it formally with wine and crystal, unleavened bread and silver. Some do it informally with grape juice and paper cups, french rolls and napkins. Some participate weekly, monthly, quarterly, annually. Some feel that the communion table is not to be celebrated at all.

Wherever, whenever and however the Lord's Table is celebrated, the believers who participate, like the disciples, enter a time machine. The bread and the wine take us back in time nearly 2000 years to Christ's sacrifice on the cross and we recall the Lord's body, mutilated and bleeding as the sacrifice for our sin. "As often as you eat this bread and drink this cup, you proclaim the Lord's death until He comes" (1 Cor. 11:26).

But the same bread and wine carry us forward in time to an event Jesus referred to when He said, "I shall never again drink of the fruit of the vine until that day when I drink it new [with you, Matt. 26:29] in the kingdom of God" (Mark 14:25). We are looking forward to the close of human history when Christ shall return to invite us to a celebration feast where we can thank Him personally for His sacrifice that provided our salvation.

135

Whether you celebrate the Lord's Table or not, it is good for us to look back to the cross and look ahead to Christ's return. Both of these events have bearing on our present life. Looking back I say, "Lord, because you were so willing to give your life for me, help me daily to give my life back to you in loving service. Let this remembrance affect my daily life."

Looking forward, I say, "Lord, the prospect of meeting you face to face encourages me to stay busy at the task of making the moments of my days count for you. I'm looking forward to your welcoming words, 'Well done!'"

May God be with you and make every communion celebration a feast you will long remember.

SCENE 36: The Big Squeeze

Read Mark 14:27-52

Shortly after graduating from Christian college I took a temporary job in a drugstore while waiting for a permanent job offer to materialize. My area of responsibility in the drugstore was the food section—stocking the shelves on the sales floor and maintaining the food section in the stockroom.

I got into a bad habit of helping myself to some of the food products while I was working in the stockroom. "I'm not stealing," I told myself. "I'm just getting rid of some of the dented cans that cannot be sold." But God shined His searchlight into my heart and helped me see that I was taking some products that could have been returned to the manufacturer for refund credit.

Once God convinced me that my snacking habit was wrong, I knew what I had to do to make it right. I had to confess my sticky-fingeredness to the store manager (who was an old friend) and pay for the goods I had consumed.

"How humiliating! How embarrassing!" I thought. "Maybe I could just slip some money into the cash register without saying anything." But my conscience would not let me off the hook. I had to confess my wrongdoing and ask forgiveness.

The day of reckoning came and I nervously asked my boss if I could speak to him. I slowly recited my well-rehearsed confession and handed him a check for an amount that covered the food I had eaten. To my relief, he not only forgave me, but tore my check in half and handed it back to me. I breathed a sigh of relief that one of the most difficult episodes in my young life was over.

Tension in the Garden

As Jesus walked into the garden of Gethsemane after sharing the Last Supper with His disciples, the painful pressure of what He knew He had to do began to show on Him. He was totally committed to doing the Father's will by giving His life to redeem lost mankind. But He was aware at the same time that this would be extremely difficult. So the tension between His commitment to do right and the pain it would bring, led Him to Gethsemane for prayer.

137

The Greek word Gethsamene means "oil press" and refers to a device that squeezes olive oil out of olives. The extracted oil was used for fueling lamps, baking bread and anointing the sick. What an appropriate place for Jesus to spend the last evening before His death. He, like the olives, was to be crushed through the experience of His crucifixion. But just as the crushed olives gave way to useful olive oil, so Christ's sacrifice provides light, nourishment and healing for our souls. In Gethsemane, Jesus felt the agonizing pressure as the hour of His rejection, trial and death drew near.

Seeing Jesus under pressure in Gethsemane encourages me, because it shows me that doing right isn't always easy, even for the Son of God. It cost Jesus plenty to go through with the Father's plan. His enemies attacked Him and His friends deserted Him. In choosing to go the Father's way, Jesus made the difficult choice of standing painfully alone.

Even today, doing what is right is not always easy or fun. For me, confessing to my boss was right, but it was anything but pleasant. It was humiliating and could have been costly had my boss not torn the check in half.

Suppose a friend passed you the answer key to tomorrow's big exam. If you hand it back you may be ridiculed by your friend for passing up such an opportunity.

Or what if, while parking your car, you crunch the taillight of another car. No one saw you, so you could leave the scene and avoid the humiliation of admitting your fault and paying for the damages. Do you do what's right even though it's more difficult? Or do you take the easy way out? Moments like that are Gethsemane experiences; times when you are under pressure to choose what's right in the face of unpleasant circumstances that may result from your choice.

A Prayer for Your Gethsemane

How can we handle the big squeeze of situations where the choice to do right leads to pain, humiliation, ostracism, or whatever? Jesus' Gethsemane prayer in Mark 14:36 is a model response—a prayer we could use in our Gethsemane experiences. Notice the four parts:

"Abba (Father)." Jesus turned to His loving Father as His resource in the midst of pressure. His heavenly Father is our heavenly Father too. The big squeeze should turn us in His direction for help.

"All things are possible for Thee." It's important to acknowledge to God that He can do *anything* He wants to do. He can eliminate any painful consequences of doing right or He can supply the strength I need to endure those consequences. It's important for us to say, "God, I know you are in control of everything."

"Remove this cup from Me." If there could have been any other way to accomplish God's plan of redemption, Jesus would have preferred it to what He faced. So we too can petition our God to change the unpleasant circumstances we face.

"Yet not what I will, but what Thou wilt." The bottom line to Jesus' prayer was resignation. That doesn't mean Jesus quit. It means that He gave Himself over to the Father's plan and promised to fulfill it even if it was not what He would wish to do. To be

139

obedient followers of Christ, we must also resign ourselves to do whatever God says is right no matter what the consequences may be.

Jesus not only prayed resignation, He lived it. Less than 24 hours after His Gethsemane prayer, His mutilated body hung limply from a bloodstained cross. Gethsemane wasn't an escape from doing right, it was necessary preparation for following through on what God confirmed was right for His Son.

The cycle isn't complete for us either until we walk out of the garden, refuse the answer key and take the exam honestly, write a note of apology and leave it with your phone number under the windshield wiper, or whatever the big squeeze dictates we must do.

SCENE 37: The Identity Crisis

Read Mark 14:53-72

Finally, they had Him.

For months the religious leaders of the Jews had been plotting some way to erase Jesus of Nazareth and His influence from among the Jewish people, but with no success. Finally they used a bag of silver coins to persuade a money-hungry disciple named Judas to betray Him to them. A mob arrested Jesus in the garden and "led Jesus away to the high priest; and all the chief priests and the elders and the scribes gathered together" (Mark 14:53). Jesus' terrified disciples evaporated into the night except for Peter, who followed at a cautious distance.

"I Am"

Once they had Jesus in hand, the Jewish leaders had a terrible time pinning a charge on Him. They brought in false witnesses against Him "yet their testimony was not consistent" (Mark 14:56).

Then the high priest stepped forward and hit the issue head-on by posing a question as to His identity as the Messiah. "Are You the Christ, the Son of the Blessed One?" (Mark 14:61). Jesus knew that an affirmative answer to this question would seal His doom, even though He was the Son of God. If Peter was near enough to hear the question the high priest asked Jesus, he was probably saying to Jesus under his breath, "Don't answer it. Say nothing at all. At least they won't be able to get you on your own confession."

But Jesus could not deny His own identity. "I am," He stated. Then He added two Old Testament quotes that further linked Him with the Messiah: "And you shall see the Son of Man sitting at the right hand of power, and coming with the clouds of heaven" (Mark 14:62, quoting Ps. 110:1 and Dan. 7:13).

Once Jesus asserted His identity as the Son of Man, the high priest was satisfied that Jesus was guilty of blasphemy, a crime punishable by death. The high priest tore his clothes (an outward sign of deep grief) and "they all condemned Him to be deserving of death" (Mark 14:64). According to John 18:31, the Sanhedrin did not have the authority to carry out a death sentence. So Jesus was bound and harassed while the Sanhedrin waited for morning when they could take Jesus before the Roman governor Pilate for sentencing.

"I Am Not"

Meanwhile out in the courtyard, another identity was on trial—that of Peter. Just a few hours earlier, Peter boldly stated, "Even though all may fall away, yet I will not" (Mark 14:29). But as Jesus faced the Sanhedrin, Peter huddled near a fire outside, perhaps with his face in the shadows, hoping to learn the fate of Jesus without being identified or implicated as His follower.

In Peter's trial, three witnesses testified spontaneously as to his identity: "You, too, were with Jesus the Nazarene" (Mark 14:67); "This is one of them!" (Mark 14:69); "Surely you are one of them, for you are a Galilean too" (Mark 14:70).

Three times Peter denied his identity as a follower of Jesus: "I neither know nor understand what you are talking about" (Mark 14:68); "Again he was denying it" (Mark 14:70); "He began to curse and swear, 'I do not know this fellow you are talking about!'" (Mark 14:71). Then a rooster's crow reminded Peter that Jesus had predicted Peter's denial the night before. Peter was destroyed with grief "and he began to weep" (Mark 14:72).

The two trials pictured in this scene remind me of the searching question you may have seen on a poster, "If you were arrested for being a Christian, would there be enough evidence to convict you?" Often our identities as believers in Christ are called into question. A friend of yours gets into some trouble and needs a Christian friend to pray and give biblical advice. You're approached by a representative from an unscriptural cult who wants you to take their literature. Or a group of Christians at your school want you to join them in sponsoring a Christian singing group at a campus outreach rally.

If you see yourself as a Christian—one who is committed to Jesus Christ and, as such, one with Him—you will step forward and be Christ's representative in each situation no matter what it might cost you. But if you see yourself as a follower of the Christian religion, the way a person might see himself as a member of a political party, you may, like Peter, avoid any visible Christian activity which may inconvenience or endanger you in some way.

Peter, of course, was rescued from the despair that characterizes him in Mark 14:72. Jesus sought him out after His resurrection and encouraged him. After the Holy Spirit descended on the day of Pentecost, Peter was a new man—he had a new identity. He was no longer a follower of Christ, he was one with Christ by the indwelling presence of Christ's Spirit. Peter's boldness on the day of Pentecost (Acts 2) was a clue to his new identity. His dynamic sermon is reminiscent of Christ when He boldly identified Himself before the Sanhedrin in Mark 14:62.

Being identified personally with Christ is what makes the difference today too, in counseling a friend, confronting a cultist or participating in an outreach rally. The old Peter will never do. The new Peter, fortified with the indwelling Christ, is needed. New Peters, like you and me, if arrested for being

Christians, wouldn't stand a chance of being acquitted.

SCENE 38: Somebody Has Taken Your Place

Read Mark 15:1-15

As the light of early morning seeped into Jerusalem, the members of the Sanhedrin led their "convicted" blasphemer Jesus to the quarters of the Roman governor of Judea, Pontius Pilate. The Jewish leaders had found Jesus guilty of blasphemy, but that charge wouldn't hold any water with the Romans who didn't even believe in the God of the Jews. So when the Sanhedrin climbed up on Pilate's porch with Jesus in tow, they inferred that Jesus was guilty of treason against Rome for calling Himself King— the King of the Jews.

Pilate's Dilemma

"Are You the King of the Jews?" (Mark 15:2) Pilate asked the question just as directly as the high priest had asked the night before. Jesus answered affirmatively. But when Pilate asked the prisoner to speak in His own defense he was dumbfounded that Jesus made no reply. Jesus, in His silence, was fulfilling the prophecy of Isaiah who said, "He was oppressed and He was afflicted, yet He did not open His mouth; like a lamb that is led to slaughter, and like a sheep that is silent before its shearer, so He did not open His mouth" (Isa. 53:7).

Pilate was in a dilemma. On one hand, he wanted to execute justice. In the case of the charges against Jesus, Pilate could find no reason for the death penalty the Sanhedrin demanded. On the other hand, Pilate wanted to please the Jews and prevent any national uprisings that might blemish his record as governor. So he kept listening to the chants of the crowd, which had been incited by the leaders, crying for Jesus' blood.

Then Pilate remembered the Passover amnesty custom. A Roman gesture of goodwill toward the Jews at Passover each year was to release one of the prisoners in the Roman jails. The governor saw the amnesty custom as a way to serve both his interests—to maintain justice and attain favor with the people. He would release Jesus as the Passover prisoner.

"Do you want me to release for you the King of the Jews?" (Mark 15:9) Pilate asked. But the well-coached crowd cried instead for the release of a murdering terrorist named Barabbas—the most notorious criminal on death row. It was unthinkable to Pilate that the Jews would call for Barabbas to be freed to run the streets again.

Pilate undoubtedly anticipated the crowd's response to his next question, but he asked it anyway. "Then what shall I do to Him whom you call the King of the Jews?" (Mark 15:12).

"Crucify Him!" began the frenzied chant. Pilate's quest for justice made one last attempt at sparing the innocent Jesus. "Why, what evil has He done?" (Mark 15:14). But the chant for Jesus' crucifixion grew until finally Pilate yielded to the crowd. "And wishing to satisfy the multitude, Pilate released Barabbas for them, and after having Jesus scourged, he delivered Him over to be crucified" (Mark 15:15).

"You're a Free Man"

"What are you doing, Roman dog?" Barabbas asked as the centurion swung open his cell door.

"You've got to be the luckiest Jew in Palestine," the centurion said with contempt as he unshackled Barabbas' hands and feet. "You're a free man, Barabbas. Somebody else will die on the cross today instead of you."

What might Barabbas have been thinking as he was escorted out of the prison gates? "Is this a trick, a joke? Are they going to do away with me outside the gate, and claim they killed me as I attempted an escape?" But the gates closed behind him and he *was* free. And a harmless Nazarene teacher was preparing to die in his place.

Do you notice any similarities between Barabbas and yourself? We have more in common with Barabbas than you might think. Barabbas had been tried, convicted and sentenced to death for murder and insurrection. He was as good as dead, sitting in his cell on death row. And he had it coming.

But in spite of his guilt, Barabbas was set free when another man, Jesus, who had committed no crime, was sentenced to the death Barabbas deserved.

I am Barabbas, and so are you. Because of the sin that infests our lives, we should be the ones walking up Golgotha to pay the death penalty sin earns ("The wages of sin is death," Rom. 6:23). But somehow, in the mystery we can only explain as God's love, we've been set free; and the only sinless man whoever lived, Jesus Christ, ended up on the cross instead. "He Himself bore our sins in His body on the cross, that we might die to sin and live to righteousness; for by His wounds we were healed" (1 Pet. 2:24).

Barabbas is never seen in Scripture again after His release from prison. I like to think that he went to Calvary while Jesus was still on the cross to see the stranger who took his death penalty. I like to imagine that Barabbas became a follower of Christ and was an active part of the early church. It just seems logical that he would have wanted to thank Jesus in some way for what He did. But the Bible is completely silent. We don't know if Barabbas was thankful or not.

Jesus to the Rescue

If my house caught fire, and my neighbor Barry pulled my family to safety but died in the process, my thankfulness for his deed would be unending.

Jesus Christ has already performed a greater rescue, and yet I'm often guilty of getting so comfortable in my salvation that I forget to express my thanks in words and deeds. Anybody want to say a personal "amen" to that?

Those of us who have personally received Christ as Saviour could spend a lifetime expressing our thanks to Jesus for taking our place on the cross—and we still would not have thanked Him adequately. But don't let that stop you. Let it encourage you to think of new ways to express your appreciation that, like Barabbas, you are free because of Christ.

Read Mark 15:16-47

One of the most dreaded punishments a prisoner can experience is solitary confinement. Being behind bars is bad enough. But being restricted from interaction with other prisoners is even worse. It's a form of discipline reserved for the most uncooperative prisoner.

During the six darkest hours in human history—the crucifixion of Jesus Christ—the King of the Jews experienced as part of His sentence the effects of solitary confinement. He was surrounded by crowds of people that day, but He was alone in the crowd with no one to help Him bear the weight of the world's sin which was nailed to the cross with Him.

The Witnesses

Look at the people who surrounded the hill of crucifixion on the day we refer to as Good Friday. There were lots of witnesses, but they stood aloof as Jesus, all alone, climaxed the work of redemption.

The Roman soldiers were there. They were the instruments used to carry out the sentence of crucifixion—a means of death so hideous that the Romans sentenced only foreign criminals to the cross, never a Roman citizen. The soldiers prepared Jesus for the cross by physically abusing Him and mocking His title—King of the Jews. Sometimes the beating suffered by a prisoner, who was sentenced to crucifixion, was so severe that he died before being spiked to the

148

cross. But Jesus survived the cruel games of the soldiers and trudged toward the cross alone.

Simon of Cyrene, North Africa, was visiting Jerusalem for the Passover when he became an unwitting part of the crucifixion drama. When Jesus buckled under the cross beam He was required to carry, Simon was drafted from the crowd to carry Jesus' load the rest of the way. Yet, even with Simon's help, Jesus staggered up Golgotha alone.

Once on the cross, Jesus' experience of physical pain and verbal abuse intensified. Agonizing hours of exposure to the elements and impaired circulation due to loss of blood caused excruciating pain for a victim of crucifixion. For Jesus, the physical pain was aggravated by the onlookers hurling abuse at Him (see Mark 15:29).

Furthermore, some of the Jewish leaders who had railroaded His crucifixion were daring Him to "come down from the cross, so that we may see and believe!" (Mark 15:32). Even the two men crucified with Him got into the act by adding their insults. Yes, the cross of Christ was encircled by people jeering and taunting Him. But He allowed His life-blood to ebb away alone.

There were people nearby who were not His enemies. The centurion in Mark 15:39 is thought to be the man in charge of the crucifixion detail. After witnessing the composure with which Jesus endured the ordeal of suffering and death, he said, "Truly this man was the Son of God!" (Mark 15:39).

Some of the women who followed Jesus and faithfully served Him in Galilee were also watching from a distance. Also watching was Joseph of Arimathea, a righteous member of the Sanhedrin who was perhaps outvoted or ignored when his fellow rulers passed sentence on Jesus. But even with friends and sympathizers present to pray and weep, Jesus approached the moment of death alone.

Completely Alone

But the climax of Jesus' isolation came during the mysterious darkness that shrouded the land from noon to 3:00. Just minutes before His last breath, Jesus' cry of despair reveals that, at that moment, He was more alone than anyone can be this side of hell: "My God, my God, why have you deserted me?" (Mark 15:34, *TLB*). Jesus was so covered with our sin that the Father turned away and Jesus suffered spiritual death—separation from God—as full payment for the sin of the human race.

"God, forsaken by God?" asked Martin Luther. "How can it be?" More brilliant minds than yours and mine have debated Luther's question and yet Jesus' cry for God is still a mystery. He was totally alone. He was separated from the Father. And then He died.

Jesus went to the cross alone so that you would never have to be alone again. That doesn't mean you will always have people around you. But it does mean that, if you're a Christian, separation from God is something you need never dread because Jesus has already received the wages your sins deserved: He experienced the hell of being separated from God.

Furthermore, you are never alone because God is with you. God the Holy Spirit is your guide, friend, counselor and teacher—your companion.

When I think of the humiliation and agony Jesus suffered on that first Good Friday, it's hard for me to understand why Jesus didn't blast His accusers and tormentors to smithereens for mistreating Him. After all, He was the God who created them. How dare they treat Him like a common criminal!

But had He not endured the pain and utter aloneness of the cross, our existence would amount to zero. Even though I can't understand why Jesus would want to take my place on the cross, I want my life to be a hymn of thankfulness and appreciation for the cross and what happened on it.

How about you?

SCENE 40: A Man of His Word

Read Mark 16:1-13

"I meant what I said, and I said what I meant; an elephant is faithful one hundred percent."

Do you recognize those immortal words? Unless you're an avid Dr. Seuss fan you probably won't be able to place the quotation. They are the words of Horton the elephant, star of one of the many Dr. Seuss stories for children. In Horton's story, a mother bird complains to Horton that she is tired of sitting on her eggs waiting for them to hatch. Softhearted Horton agrees to take her place on the nest while the mother bird flies off for a brief vacation.

Many days pass while Horton keeps his vigil atop the nest. Numerous opportunities and temptations encourage him to forsake his post, but each time he responds firmly with his words of commitment: "I meant what I said and I said what I meant; an elephant is faithful one hundred percent."

Finally the mother bird returns to the nest, Horton is relieved and the baby birds are hatched. The moral of the story is that a person, like Horton, should be faithful to do what he says he will do. It is a point well taken, for most of us have a hard time staying true to our word most of the time, let alone "one hundred percent."

Mark 16 opens with the good news that Jesus Christ "meant what He said, and said what He meant" about coming back to life after His crucifixion. As chapter 15 closed, the battered body of Jesus was being hastily wrapped in a linen sheet and sealed in a tomb. There was not even time to prepare His body properly for burial because sundown began the Sabbath on which no work was to be done.

From the disciples' point of view, things looked darker than the inside of the tomb after the stone had been rolled into place. Their hopes of ruling with the Messiah on earth had been smashed. Their authoritative and loving teacher had been stolen from among them and brutally murdered. And now they huddled in hiding for fear that they too would be the victims of the outrage which resulted in Jesus' death. There is absolutely no evidence in Scripture that suggests the disciples either remembered or believed Jesus' prediction in Mark 9:31 that He would rise again. The bottom had dropped out of their world and they were "mourning and weeping" (Mark 16:10) their fate.

A few of the women who had followed Jesus arrived at the tomb early Sunday morning to pay Him final tribute. Since Jesus had been hurriedly sealed in the tomb without the customary embalming process, the women "bought spices, that they might come and anoint Him" (Mark 16:1).

When the women arrived at the tomb, they were astonished to find the huge stone rolled away from the entrance, Jesus' body missing and an angelic figure waiting for them. "And he said to them, 'Do not be amazed; you are looking for Jesus the Nazarene, who has been crucified. He has risen; He is not here; behold, here is the place where they laid Him. But go, tell His disciples and Peter, "He is going before you into Galilee; there you will see Him, *just as He said to you*"'" (Mark 16:6,7, italics added).

It's interesting to me that the angel would add the six-word zinger onto the end of his speech. Jesus evidently wanted His disciples to be reminded that everything was happening according to the plan He outlined for them beforehand. The disciples had forgotten that Jesus had prearranged their post-resurrection meeting place when He said, "After I have been raised, I will go before you to Galilee" (Matt. 26:32).

True to form, when the disciples heard what the angels told the women, "they refused to believe it" (Mark 16:11). Even after two of the men reported seeing the risen Christ, the rest of the disciples "did not believe them either" (Mark 16:13). But let's not be too hard on these men. You and I probably would have held the same attitude under those circumstances.

Have you ever stopped to think what it would be like for us if Jesus had not come back to life and the Gospel of Jesus Christ had ended with Mark 15? For openers, we would have to throw out the entire Bible. After all, if Jesus had been unable to fulfill His prediction of resurrection on the third day, then God's Word would not be trustworthy and we could expect other disappointing inconsistencies.

Furthermore, we would abandon our Christian lifestyle and stop struggling against the sin nature that so desperately wants to reclaim each believer. For if Jesus was unable to conquer death, it is certain that none of us has the capacity to bring ourselves back to life. And with no hope for life after death, we might as well join the rest of the world in making pleasure our god and grabbing for all the gusto we can in our short existence.

The apostle Paul summarized how futile life would be without the hope of resurrection that Christ provided when He crumbled the chains of death and emerged from the tomb alive: "If he [Christ] is still dead, then all our preaching is useless and your trust in God is empty, worthless, hopeless .... And if being a Christian is of value to us only now in this life, we are the most miserable of creatures" (1 Cor. 15: 14,19, *TLB*).

But the heart of the good news we call the gospel is that Jesus meant what He said, and said what He meant; the Saviour was faithful one hundred percent. He promised His disciples that death would not keep Him down. And even though their despair obliterat-

154

ed Jesus' prophecy of resurrection from their minds, He *did* come back alive from the dead "just as He said" (Mark 16:7).

Jesus has a perfect track record as far as doing what He said He would do. That truth has dynamic implications for you and me. When Christ says to us through the Scriptures, "I am with you always" (Matt. 28:20) and "God causes all things to work together for good" (Rom. 8:28), He meant what He said! He has never failed to keep a promise yet. Every promise in Scripture is given by a Person who keeps His Word. You can bank on it.

SCENE 41: There's Good News and There's Bad News

Read Mark 16:14-20

Having preached a few sermons in my day, I have a great appreciation for zippy sermon titles, the kind that grab people's attention and invite them to lean forward and listen. For example, a sermon on the difficulties of disciplining the tongue entitled "Bible Principles for Exemplary Christian Speech" doesn't grab me. But if the same topic were titled, "Loose Lips Sink Ships" I would be much more interested and ready to listen.

The sermon title that gets my trophy for being the most inventive and attention-getting was on the announcement board in front of an evangelical church in San Diego, California. It read something like this: "Every Member of This Church Ought to GO TO HELL!" If I had been a member of that church I would have been sitting front-row center that Sunday to hear the preacher explain the meaning of that eyebrow-raising title. As it turned out, the urgent message the minister conveyed in his sermon was this: if every church member had firsthand knowledge of what hell is like, they would be more aggressive about warning people who are headed that way.

There is a similar note of urgency in Jesus' final message to His disciples as recorded in Mark 16:14-20. In harmony with his style throughout the Gospel, Mark condenses Jesus' last 40 days on earth into only a few verses and summarizes His last words into one brief monologue.

This Is the Beginning

The essence of Jesus' parting words to His disciples is the command in Mark 16:15, "Go into all the world and preach the gospel to all creation." The resurrection of Jesus Christ from the grave might have seemed to the disciples like a happy ending to the story of their Master's life. But Jesus' command informed them that the resurrection was not the end —it was just the beginning! The events and meaning of Christ's life, death and resurrection were the essential ingredients to the message the disciples (and subsequent followers of Christ like us) were to take around the world.

In addition to His basic command to spread the gospel, Jesus added some good news and some bad news in Mark 16:16. First the good news: "He who has believed and has been baptized shall be saved." That's not just good news, that's *great* news! Any person anywhere in the world who gives himself to God through faith in Jesus Christ is rescued from the power and penalty of sin. The offer was not restricted to the disciples, or to Jews, or to Anglo-Saxon Protestants. It was a blank check signed by Jesus and offered to "he who believes" in "all the world."

There is some difference of opinion among believers as to how verses 17 and 18 are to be interpreted. Some feel that these attesting miracles were only to be present during the ministry of the apostles in the first-century church. Others feel that they continue throughout the church age. But the lowest common denominator for these verses is the truth that God's power is present with each believer to equip him or her to live the Christian life and communicate it to others. And that's great news too.

Save the Condemned

But there is also some bad news in Mark 16:16: "He who has disbelieved shall be condemned." Even though the gospel of Jesus Christ is the greatest news to be announced to the human race, some people will refuse to believe it. And those who disbelieve the gospel are sentenced to spend eternity separated from the God whose gift of salvation they have refused. That's *terrible* news.

God hates the bad news even more than you do. That's why Mark 16:15 is in the Bible. He has charged His followers to spread the good news by the power of His indwelling Spirit so that many more of

157

those in the "condemned" category might believe in Christ and transfer into the "saved" category.

You might think, as I once did, that Mark 16:15 is telling every Christian to sign up as a "hellfire and brimstone" street-corner evangelist, a pulpit-pounding preacher or a missionary to demon-possessed headhunters. But preaching the gospel has a much broader application than the three kinds of preachers just mentioned. For you, preaching the gospel may mean telling an unbelieving friend about what Christ has done in your life, leading an evangelistic campus Bible study, or participating in a door-to-door visitation program sponsored by your church. The idea is to let your friends and classmates know that there is good news to be heard and received. The rest is up to God and the individual.

There are a lot of people in your world who are "condemned" because they have not heard, understood or received the good news about salvation through Christ. You could spend your days running through the halls at school screaming, "You're condemned and you're going to hell unless you get saved!" at the top of your lungs. But more realistically, you could patiently and consistently share Christ as you know Him to anyone who will listen.

When I was in high school, my friend Bob was among the "condemned." I was no polished evangelist or flawless witness, but over the span of about four years Bob was drawn to Christ through my efforts. Today Bob is the pastor of a church. Believe me, if God could use my feeble "preaching" to win my friend, He can use you to win anybody.

Shortly after Jesus commissioned the disciples He

was taken up in the clouds. Mark concludes his Gospel by telling us that the disciples "went out and preached everywhere, while the Lord worked with them" (Mark 16:20). Each succeeding generation of believers has obeyed the command to share the good news. That's how the gospel has come to you. Now it's your turn to pass it on. But as you do, keep one eye on the clouds. Because here comes Jesus again.